THE DHAMMAPADA

A COLLECTON OF VERSES

THE DHAMMAPADA

A COLLECTON OF VERSES

VOL-X

PART -I

BEING ONE OF THE CANONICAL BOOKS OF THE

BUDDHISTS

TRANSLATED FROM PALI

BY

F. MAX MULLER

ISBN: 978-93-5128-722-3

First Published in 1881
Indian Reprint in 2017

Published by

Kalpaz Publications
C-30, Satyawati Nagar,
Delhi – 110052
E-mail: kalpaz@hotmail.com
Website: kalpazpublications.com
Ph.: +91-9212142040

Cataloging in Publication Data—DK
Courtesy: D.K. Agencies (P) Ltd. <docinfo@dkagencies.com>

Tipitòaka. Suttapitòaka. Khuddakanika˜ya. Dhammapada. English.
The Dhammapada : a collection of verses : being one of the canonical books of the Buddhists / translated from Pali by F. Max Muller.
    pages cm. — ([Sacred books of the East] ; vol-X, part-I)
"First published in 1881"—Title page verso.
ISBN 9789351287223

    1. Buddhism—Sacred books.   I. Mu˜ller, F. Max (Friedrich Max), 1823-1900, translator. II. Title.   III. Series: Sacred books of the East ; vol-X, part-I.

BQ1138.T57 2017   DDC 294.382   23

THE DHAMMAPADA

A COLLECTION OF VERSES

Is the part of

SACRED BOOKS OF THE EAST

CONTENTS.

INTRODUCTION

TO

THE DHAMMAPADA.

The Dhammapada, a Canonical Book.

THE Dhammapada forms part of the Pâli Buddhist canon,
though its exact place varies according to different authorities, and we have not as yet a sufficient number of complete
MSS. of the Tipitaka to help us to decide the question [1].
Those who divide that canon into three Pitakas or
baskets, the Vinaya-pitaka, Sutta-pitaka, and Abhidham-
ma-pitaka, assign the Dhammapada to the Sutta-pitaka.
That Pitaka consists of five Nikâyas: the Dîgha-nikâya,
the Magghima-nikâya, the Samyutta-nikâya, the Anguttara-
nikâya, and the Khuddaka-nikâya. The fifth, or Khuddaka-
nikâya, comprehends the following works: 1. Khuddaka-
pâtha; 2. DHAMMAPADA; 3. Udâna; 4. Itivuttaka; 5. Suttanipâta; 6. Vimânavatthu; 7. Petavatthu; 8. Theragâthâ;
9. Therîgâthâ; 10. Gâtaka; 11. Niddesa; 12. Patisambhidâ;
13. Apadâna; 14. Buddhavamsa; 15. Kariyâ-pitaka.

According to another division [2], however, the whole Buddhist canon consists of five Nikâyas: the Dîgha-nikâya, the
Magghima-nikâya, the Samyutta-nikâya, the Anguttara-
nikâya, and the fifth, the Khuddaka-nikâya, which Khuddaka-nikâya is then made to comprehend the whole of
the Vinaya (discipline) and Abhidhamma (metaphysics),
together with the fifteen books beginning with the Khud-
daka-pâtha.

The order of these fifteen books varies, and even, as
it would seem, their number. The Dîghabhânaka school

---

[1] See Feer, Journal Asiatique, 1871, p. 263. There is now at least one com-
plete MS. of the Tipitaka, the Phayre MS., at the India Office, and Professor
Forchhammer has just published a most useful List of Pâli MSS., collected in
Burma, the largest collection hitherto known.

[2] See Childers, s. v. Nikâya, and extracts from Buddhaghosa's commentary
on the Brahmagâla-sutta.

admits twelve books only, and assigns them all to the Abhidhamma, while the Ma*gghi*mabhâ*n*akas admit fifteen books,
and assign them to the Sutta-pi*t*aka. The order of the
fifteen books is : 1. *G*âtaka [10]; 2. Mahâniddesa [11];
3. *K*ullaniddesa [11]; 4. Pa*t*isambhidâmagga [12]; 5. Suttanipâta [5]; 6. DHAMMAPADA [2]; 7. Udâna [3]; 8. Itivuttaka [4]; 9. Vimânavatthu [6]; 10. Petavatthu [7];
11. Theragâthâ [8]; 12. Therîgâthâ [9]; 13. *K*ariyâpi*t*aka [15]; 14. Apadâna [13]; 15. Buddhava*m*sa [14] [1].

The Khuddaka-pâ*th*a is left out in the second list, and
the number is brought to fifteen by dividing Niddesa into
Mahâ-niddesa and *K*ulla-niddesa.

There is a commentary on the Dhammapada in Pâli,
and supposed to be written by Buddhaghosa [2], in the first
half of the fifth century A.D. In explaining the verses of the
Dhammapada, the commentator gives for every or nearly
every verse a parable to illustrate its meaning, which is
likewise believed to have been uttered by Buddha in his
intercourse with his disciples, or in preaching to the multi-
tudes that came to hear him.

DATE OF THE DHAMMAPADA.

The only means of fixing the date of the Dhammapada
is trying to ascertain the date of the Buddhist canon
of which it forms a part, or the date of Buddhaghosa,
who wrote a commentary on it. This, however, is by no
means easy, and the evidence on which we have to rely is
such that we must not be surprised if those who are
accustomed to test historical and chronological evidence

---

[1] The figures within brackets refer to the other list of books in the Khuddaka-nikâya. See also p. xxviii.

[2] M. Léon Feer in the Journal Asiatique, 1871, p. 266, mentions another commentary of a more philosophical character, equally ascribed to Buddhaghosa,
and having the title Vivara Bra Dhammapada, i. e. L'auguste Dhammapada
dévoilé. Professor Forchhammer in his ' List of Manuscripts,' 1879–80, mentions the following works in connection with the Dhammapada : Dhammapada-
Nissayo; Dh. P. A*tth*akathâ by Buddhaghosa; Dh. P. A*tth*akathâ Nissayo,
3 vols., containing a complete translation of the commentary; Dh. P. Va*tth*u.
Of printed books he quotes: Kayanupassanakyam, a work based on the
*G*arâvaggo, Mandalay, 1876 (390 pages), and Dhammapada-desanakyam,
printed in ' British Burma News.'

in Greece and Rome, decline to be convinced by it. As a general rule, I quite agree that we cannot be too sceptical in assigning a date to ancient books, particularly if we intend to use them as documents for tracing the history of human thought. To the initiated, I mean to those who have themselves worked in the mines of ancient Oriental literature, such extreme scepticism may often seem unscientific and uncalled for. They are more or less aware of hundreds of arguments, each by itself, it may be, of small weight, but all combined proving irresistible. They are conscious, too, of having been constantly on the look out for danger, and, as all has gone on smoothly, they feel sure that, in the main, they are on the right road. Still it is always useful to be as incredulous as possible, particularly against oneself, and to have before our eyes critics who will not yield one inch beyond what they are forced to yield by the strongest pressure of facts.

The age of our MSS. of the canonical books, either in Pâli or Sanskrit, is of no help to us. All Indian MSS. are comparatively modern, and one who has probably handled more Indian MSS. than anybody else, Mr. A. Burnell, has lately expressed his conviction that 'no MS. written one thousand years ago is now existent in India, and that it is almost impossible to find one written five hundred years ago, for most MSS. which claim to be of that date are merely copies of old MSS. the dates of which are repeated by the copyists[1].'

Nor is the language, whether Sanskrit or Pâli, a safe guide for fixing dates. Both languages continue to be written to our own time, and though there are some characteristic marks to distinguish more modern from more ancient Buddhist Sanskrit and Pâli, this branch of critical scholarship requires to be cultivated far more extensively and accurately before true scholars would venture to fix the date of a Sanskrit or Pâli text on the strength of linguistic evidence alone[2].

---

[1] Indian Antiquary, 1880, p. 233.
[2] See some important remarks on this subject in Fausböll's Introduction to Sutta-nipâta, p. xi.

The Buddhists themselves have no difficulty in assigning a date to their sacred canon. They are told in that canon itself that it was settled at the First Council, or immediately after the death of Buddha, and they believe that it was afterwards handed down by means of oral tradition, or actually written down in books by order of Kâ*s*yapa, the president of the First Council [1]. Buddhaghosa, a learned and in some respects a critical scholar, living in the beginning of the fifth century A.D., asserts that the canon which he had before him, was the same as that fixed by the First Council [2].

Several European students have adopted the same opinion, and, so far as I know, no argument has yet been advanced showing the impossibility of the native view, that some collection of Buddha's doctrines was made immediately after his death at Râ*g*agaha, and that it was finally settled at what is called the Second Council, or the Council of Vesâlî. But what is not impossible is not therefore true, nor can anything be gained by appealing to later witnesses, such as, for instance, Hiouen Thsang, who travelled through India in the seventh century, and wrote down anything that he could learn, little concerned whether one statement tallied with the other or not [3]. He says that the Tipi*t*aka was written down on palm leaves by Kâ*s*yapa at the end of the First Council. But what can be the weight of such a witness, living more than a thousand years after the event, compared with that, for instance, of the Mahâvam sa, which dates from the fifth century of our era, and

---

[1] Bigandet, Life of Gaudama (Rangoon, 1866), p. 350 ; but also p. 120 note.

[2] See Childers, s. v. Tipi*t*aka. There is a curious passage in Buddhaghosa's account of the First Council. ' Now one may ask,' he says, ' Is there or is there not in this first Parâ*g*ika anything to be taken away or added?' I reply, There is nothing in the words of the Blessed Buddha that can be taken away, for the Buddhas speak not even a single syllable in vain, yet in the words of disciples and devatâs there are things which may be omitted, and these the elders who made the recension, did omit. On the other hand, additions are everywhere necessary, and accordingly, whenever it was necessary to add anything, they added it. If it be asked, What are the additions referred to ? I reply, Only sentences necessary to connect the text, as 'at that time,' 'again at that time,' 'and so forth.'

[3] Pèlerins Bouddhistes, vol. i. p. 158.

tells us in the account of Mahinda's missionary journey to Ceylon (241/318), that the son of Asoka had to spend three years in learning the Tipitaka by heart from the mouth of a teacher[1]? No mention is then made of any books or MSS., when it would have been most natural to do so[2]. At a later time, during the reign of King Vattagâmani[3] (88–76 B.C.), the same chronicle, the Mahavamsa, tells us that 'the profoundly wise priests had theretofore orally (mukhapâthena) perpetuated the Pâli of the Pitakattaya and its Atthakathâ (commentary), but that at this period the priests, foreseeing the perdition of the people assembled, and in order that the religion might endure for ages, recorded the same in books (potthakesu likhâpayum)[4].'

No one has yet questioned the dates of the Dîpavamsa, about 400 A.D., or of the first part of the Mahâvamsa, between 459–477 A. D., and though no doubt there is an interval of nearly 600 years between the composition of the Mahâvamsa and the recorded writing down of the Buddhist canon under Vattagâmani, yet we must remember that the Ceylonese chronicles were confessedly founded on an older Atthakathâ preserved in the monasteries of the island, and representing an unbroken line of local tradition.

My own argument therefore, so long as the question was only whether we could assign a pre-Christian date to the Pâli Buddhist canon, has always been this. We have the commentaries on the Pâli canon translated from Sinhalese into Pâli, or actually composed, it may be, by Buddhaghosa. Buddhaghosa confessedly consulted various

---

[1] Mahâvamsa, p. 37; DîpavamsaVII, 28–31; Buddhaghosha's Parables, p. xviii.

[2] Bigandet, Life of Gaudama, p. 351.

[3] Dr. E. Müller (Indian Antiquary, Nov. 1880, p. 270) has discovered inscriptions in Ceylon, belonging to Devanapiya Maharâga Gâmini Tissa, whom he identifies with Vattagâmani.

[4] The same account is given in the Dîpavamsa XX, 20, and in the Sârasangraha, as quoted by Spence Hardy, Legends, p. 192. As throwing light on the completeness of the Buddhist canon at the time of King Vattagâmani, it should be mentioned that, according to the commentary on the Mahâvamsa (Turnour, p. liii), the sect of the Dhammarukikas established itself at the Abhayavihâra, which had been constructed by Vattagâmani, and that one of the grounds of their secession was their refusing to acknowledge the Parivâra (thus I read instead of Pariwâna) as part of the Vinaya-pitaka. According to the Dîpavamsa (VII, 42) Mahinda knew the Parivâra.

MSS., and gives various readings, just as any modern scholar might do. This was in the beginning of the fifth century A.D., and there is nothing improbable, though I would say no more, in supposing that some of the MSS., consulted by Buddhaghosa, dated from the first century B.C., when Va*tt*agâmani ordered the sacred canon to be reduced to writing.

There is one other event with reference to the existence of the sacred canon in Ceylon, recorded in the Mahâva*m*sa, between the time of Buddhaghosa and Va*tt*agâmani, viz. the translation of the Suttas from Pâli into the language of Ceylon, during the reign of Buddhadâsa, 339–368 A. D. If MSS. of that ancient translation still existed, they would, no doubt, be very useful for determining the exact state of the Pâli originals at that time [1]. But even without them there seems no reason to doubt that Buddhaghosa had before him old MSS. of the Pâli canon, and that these were in the main the same as those written down at the time of Va*tt*agâmani.

BUDDHAGHOSA'S AGE.

The whole of this argument, however, rested on the supposition that Buddhaghosa's date in the beginning of the fifth century A.D. was beyond the reach of reasonable doubt. 'His age,' I had ventured to say in the Preface to Buddhaghosha's Parables (1870), 'can be fixed with greater accuracy than most dates in the literary history of India.' But soon after, one of our most celebrated Pâli scholars, the great Russian traveller, Professor Joh. Minayeff, expressed in the Mélanges Asiatiques (13/25 April, 1871) the gravest doubts as to Buddhaghosa's age, and thus threw the whole Buddhist chronology, so far as it had then been accepted by all, or nearly all scholars, back into chaos. He gave as his chief reason that Buddhaghosa was not, as I supposed, the contemporary of Mahânâma, the

---

[1] A note is added, stating that several portions of the other two divisions also of the Pi*t*akattaya were translated into the Sinhalese language, and that these alone are consulted by the priests, who are unacquainted with Pâli. On the other hand, it is stated that the Sinhalese text of the A*tth*akathâ exists no longer. See Spence Hardy, Legends, p. xxv, and p. 69.

author of the Mahâvamsa, but of another Mahânâma, the king of Ceylon.

Professor Minayeff is undoubtedly right in this, but I am not aware that I, or anybody else, had ever questioned so palpable a fact. There are two Mahânâmas ; one, the king who reigned from 410–432 A.D. ; the other, the supposed author of the Mahâvamsa, the uncle and protector of King Dhâtusena, 459–477. ' Dhâtusena,' I had written, 'was the nephew of the historian Mahânâma, and owed the throne to the protection of his uncle. Dhâtusena was in fact the restorer of a national dynasty, and after having defeated the foreign usurpers (the Damilo dynasty) "he restored the religion which had been set aside by the foreigners"' (Mahâv. p. 256). Among his many pious acts it is particularly mentioned that he gave a thousand, and ordered the Dîpavamsa to be promulgated. As Mahânâma was the uncle of Dhâtusena, who reigned from 459–477, he may be considered as a trustworthy witness with regard to events that occurred between 410 and 432. Now the literary activity of Buddhaghosa in Ceylon falls in that period[1].'

These facts being admitted, it is surely not too great a stretch of probability to suppose, as I did, that a man whose nephew was king in 459–477, might have been alive in 410–432, that is to say, might have been a contemporary of Buddhaghosa. I did not commit myself to any further theories. The question whether Mahânâma, the uncle of Dhâtusena, was really the author of the Mahâvamsa, the question whether he wrote the second half of the 37th chapter of that work, or broke off his chronicle in the middle of that chapter, I did not discuss, having no new materials to bring forward beyond those on which Turnour and those who followed him had founded their conclusions, and which I had discussed in my History of Sanskrit Literature (1859), p. 267. All I said was, ' It is difficult to determine whether the 38th as well as the (whole of the) 37th chapter came from the pen of Mahânâma, for

---

[1] 'Ungefähr 50 Jahre älter als Mahânâma ist Buddhaghosha,' see Westergaard, Über Buddha's Todesjahr, p. 99.

the Mahâvamsa was afterwards continued by different
writers, even to the middle of the last century. But,
taking into account all the circumstances of the case, it is
most probable that Mahânâma carried on the history to
his own time, to the death of Dhâtusena, 477 A.D.'
What I meant by 'all the circumstances of the case'
might easily be understood by any one who had read Turnour's Preface to the Mahâvamsa. Turnour himself thought
at first that Mahânâma's share in the Mahâvamsa ended
with the year 301 A.D., and that the rest of the work, called
the Sulu Wansé, was composed by subsequent writers[1].
Dharmakîrti is mentioned by name as having continued
the work to the reign of Prâkrama Bâhu (A.D. 1266). But
Turnour afterwards changed his mind[2]. Considering that
the account of Mahâsena's reign, the first of the Seven
Kings, terminates in the middle of a chapter, at verse 48,
while the whole chapter is called the Sattarâgiko, 'the
chapter of the Seven Kings,' he naturally supposed that
the whole of that chapter, extending to the end of the reign
of his nephew Dhâtusena, might be the work of Mahânâma,
unless there were any strong proofs to the contrary. Such
proofs, beyond the tradition of writers of the MSS., have
not, as yet, been adduced[3].

But even if it could be proved that Mahânâma's own pen
did not go beyond the 48th verse of the 37th chapter, the
historical trustworthiness of the concluding portion of that
chapter, containing the account of Buddhaghosa's literary
activity, nay, even of the 38th chapter, would be little
affected thereby. We know that both the Mahâvamsa
and the somewhat earlier Dîpavamsa were founded on the
Sinhalese Atthakathâs, the commentaries and chronicles
preserved in the Mahâvihâra at Anurâdhapura. We also
know that that Vihâra was demolished by Mahâsena, and
deserted by nearly all its inmates for the space of nine
years (p. 235), and again for the space of nine months

---

[1] Introduction, p. ii. The Kûlavamsa is mentioned with the Mahâvamsa, both
as the works of Mahânâma, by Professor Forchhammer in his List of Pâli MSS.
[2] Introduction, p. xci.
[3] See Rhys Davids, Journal of the Royal Asiatic Society, 1875, p. 196.

(p. 237). We can well understand therefore why the older history, the Dîpavaṃsa, should end with the death of Mahâsena (died 302 A.D.), and why in the Mahâvaṃsa too there should have been a break at that date. But we must not forget that, during Mahânâma's life, the Mahâvihâra at Anurâdhapura was restored, that some kind of chronicle, called the Dîpavaṃsa, whether it be a general name of any ' chronicle of the island,' or of our Dîpavaṃsa, or, it may be, even of our Mahâvaṃsa, was ordered to be published or promulgated (dîpetum)under Dhâtusena,the nephew and protegé of Mahânâma. Therefore, even if we do not insist on the personal authorship of Mahânâma, we may certainly maintain that historical entries had been made in the chronicles of Anurâdhapura during Dhâtusena's reign, and probably under the personal auspices of Mahânâma, so that if we find afterwards, in the second half of the 37th chapter of his Mahâvaṃsa, an account of events which had happened between the destruction of the Mahâvihâra and the reign of Dhâtusena, and among them an account of so important an event as the arrival of Buddhaghosa from Magadha and his translation of the Sinhalese Aṭṭhakathâ into the language of Magadha, we may well suppose that they rest on the authority of native chronicles, written not long after the events, and that therefore, ' under all the circumstances of the case,' the age of Buddhaghosa can be fixed with greater accuracy than most dates in the literary history of India.

There is one difficulty still remaining with regard to the date of the historian Mahânâma which might have perplexed Turnour's mind, and has certainly proved a stumbling-block to myself. Turnour thought that the author of the commentary oñ the Mahâvaṃsa, the Vaṃsatthappakâsinî, was the same as the author of the Mahâvaṃsa, viz. Mahânâma. The date of that commentary, however, as we know now, must be fixed much later, for it speaks of a schism which took place in the year 601 A.D., during the reign of Agrabôdhi (also called Dhâtâpatisso). Turnour[1] looked

---

[1] Introduction, p. liii.

[10]   b

upon that passage as a later interpolation, because he thought the evidence for the identity of the author and the commentator of the Mahâvamsa too strong to be set aside. He trusted chiefly to a passage in the commentary, and if that passage had been correctly rendered, the conclusion which he drew from it could hardly be resisted. We read in the Mahâvamsa (p. 254):

'Certain members of the Moriyan dynasty, dreading the power of the (usurper) Subho, the bâlattho, had settled in various parts of the country, concealing themselves. Among them there was a certain landed proprietor Dhâtusena, who had established himself at Nandivâpi. His son named Dhâtâ, who lived at the village Ambiliyâgo, had two sons, Dhâtusena and Sîlatissabodhi, of unexceptional descent. Their mother's brother (Mahânâma), devoted to the cause of religion, continued to reside (at Anurâdhapura) in his sacerdotal character, at the edifice built by the minister Dîghasandana. The youth Dhâtusena became a priest in his fraternity, and on a certain day, while he was chaunting at the foot of a tree, a shower of rain fell, and a Nâga, seeing him there, encircled him in his folds, and covered him and his book with his hood. . . . Causing an image of Mahâ Mahinda to be made, and conveying it to the edifice (Ambamâlaka) in which the thera's body had been burnt, in order that he might celebrate a great festival there, and that he might also promulgate the contents of the Dîpavamsa, distributing a thousand pieces, he caused it to be read aloud[1].'

If we compare with this extract from the Mahâvamsa a passage from the commentary as translated by Turnour, we can well understand how he arrived at the conclusion that it was written by the same person who wrote the Mahâvamsa.

Turnour translates (p. liv):

'Upon these data by me, the thera, who had, with due

---

[1] Mr. Turnour added a note in which he states that Dîpavamsa is here meant for Mahâvamsa, but whether brought down to this period, or only to the end of the reign of Mahâsena, to which alone the Tîkâ extends, there is no means of ascertaining (p. 257).

solemnity, been invested with the dignified title of Mahâ-nâma, resident at the pariveṇa founded by the minister Dîghasandana, endowed with the capacity requisite to record the narrative comprised in the Mahâvaṃsa, in due order, rejecting only the dialect in which the Singhalese Aṭṭhakathâ are written, but retaining their import and following their arrangement, the history, entitled the Palapadôruvaṃsa (Padyapadânuvaṃsa), is compiled. As even in times when the despotism of the ruler of the land, and the horrors arising from the inclemencies of the seasons, and when panics of epidemics and other visitations prevailed, this work escaped all injury; and moreover, as it serves to perpetuate the fame of the Buddhas, their disciples, and the Paché Buddhas of old, it is also worthy of bearing the title of Vaṃsatthappakâsinî.'

As the evidence of these two passages in support of the identity of the author and the commentator of the Mahâvaṃsa seemed to me very startling, I requested Mr. Rhys Davids to copy for me the passage of the commentary.

The passage runs as follows :

Yâ ettavatâ mahâvaṃsatthânusârakusalena Dîghasanda-senâpatinâ kârâpita-mahâpariveṇavâsinâ Mahânâmo ti ga-rûhi gahitanâmadheyyena thereṇa pubba-Sîhala-bhâsitâya Sîhalaṭṭhakathâya bhâsantaraṃ eva vaggiya atthasâram eva gahetva tantinayânurûpena katassa imassa Padyapadâ-nuvaṃsassa atthavaṇṇanâ mayâ tam eva sannissitena âraddhâ, padesissariya-dubbuṭṭhibhaya-rogabhayâdi-vivi-dha-antarâya-yuttakâle pi anantarâyena niṭṭhânam upagatâ, sâ buddha-buddhasâvaka-pakkekabuddhâdînaṃ porâṇânaṃ kikkaṃ pubbavaṃsatthappakâsanato ayaṃ Vaṃsatthappa-kâsinî nâmâ ti dhâretabbâ. . . . Padyapadânuvaṃsa-vaṇṇanâ Vaṃsatthappakâsinî niṭṭhitâ.

Mr. Rhys Davids translates this :

' The commentary on this Padyapadânuvaṃsa, which (latter work) was made (in the same order and arrangement, and re-taining the sense, but rejecting the dialect, of the Sinhalese commentary formerly expressed in the Sinhalese tongue) by the elder who bore the name of Mahânâma, which he had

received from the venerable, who resided at the Mahâpari-
ve*n*a built by the minister Dîghasanda, and who was well
able to conform to the sense of the Mahâva*m*sa—(this commentary) which was undertaken by me out of devotion to
that (history), and which (though thus undertaken) at a time
full of danger of various kinds—such as the danger from
disease, and the danger from drought, and the danger
from the government of the province—has been safely
brought to a conclusion—this (commentary), since it makes
known the meaning of the history of old, the mission of
the ancients, of the Buddhas, of their disciples, and of the
Pa*kk*eka Buddhas, should bear the name Va*m*satthappa-
kâsinî. . . .

     'End of the Va*m*satthappakâsinî, the commentary on
          the Padyapadânuva*m*sa.'

    This shows clearly that Turnour made a mistake in trans-
lating this exceedingly involved, yet perfectly intelligible,
passage, and that so far from proving that the author of
the commentary was the same person as the author of the
text [1], it proves the very contrary. Nay, I feel bound to
add, that we might now argue that as the commentator
must have lived later than 601 A. D., the fact that he too
breaks off at verse 48 of chapter 37, seems to show that at
his time also the Mahâva*m*sa did not extend as yet beyond
that verse. But even then, the fact that with the restoration
of the Mahâvihâra of Anurâdhapura an interest in historical
studies revived in Ceylon, would clearly show that we may
trust the date of Buddhaghosa, as fixed by the second part
of the 37th chapter of the Mahâva*m*sa, at all events till
stronger evidence is brought forward against such a date.
    Now I am not aware of any such evidence [2]. On the
contrary, making allowance for a difference of some ten or
twenty years, all the evidence which we can gain from
other quarters tends to confirm the date of Buddha-

    [1] Dr. Oldenberg informs me that the commentator quotes various readings
in the text of the Mahâva*m*sa.
    [2] The passage, quoted by Professor Minayeff from the Sâsanava*m*sa, would
assign to Buddhaghosa the date of 930 − 543 = 387 A.D., which can easily be
reconciled with his accepted date. If he is called the contemporary of Siripâla,
we ought to know who that Siripâla is.

ghosa[1]. I therefore feel no hesitation in here reprinting that story, as we find it in the Mahâvamsa, not free from legendary ingredients, it is true, yet resting, I believe, on a sound foundation of historical fact.

'A Brâhman youth, born in the neighbourhood of the terrace of the great Bo-tree (in Magadha), accomplished in the "viggâ" (knowledge) and "sippa" (art), who had achieved the knowledge of the three Vedas, and possessed great aptitude in attaining acquirements; indefatigable as a schismatic disputant, and himself a schismatic wanderer over Gambudîpa, established himself, in the character of a disputant, in a certain vihâra[2], and was in the habit of rehearsing, by night and by day with clasped hands, a discourse which he had learned, perfect in all its component parts, and sustained throughout in the same lofty strain. A certain Mahâthera, Revata, becoming acquainted with him there, and (saying to himself), "This individual is a person of profound knowledge, it will be worthy (of me) to convert him;" enquired, "Who is this who is braying like an ass?" The Brâhman replied to him, "Thou canst define, then, the meaning conveyed in the bray of asses." On the Thera rejoining, "I can define it;" he (the Brâhman) exhibited the extent of the knowledge he possessed. The Thera criticised each of his propositions, and pointed out in what respect they were fallacious. He who had been thus refuted, said, "Well, then, descend to thy own creed;" and he propounded to him a passage from the Abhidhamma (of the Pitakattaya). He (the Brâhman) could not divine the signification of that passage, and enquired, "Whose manta is this?"—"It is Buddha's manta." On his exclaiming, "Impart it to me;" the Thera replied, "Enter the sacerdotal order." He who was desirous of acquiring the knowledge of the Pitakattaya, subsequently coming to this conviction, "This is the sole road" (to salvation), became a convert to that faith. As he was as profound in his eloquence (ghosa) as Buddha himself, they conferred on him the appellation of Buddhaghosa (the

---

[1] See Bigandet, Life of Gaudama, pp. 351, 381.

[2] On this vihâra, its foundation and character, see Oldenberg, Vinaya, vol. i. p. liii; Hiouen-thsang, III, p. 487 seq.

voice of Buddha); and throughout the world he became as
renowned as Buddha. Having there (in Gambudîpa) composed an original work called Ñânodaya (Rise of Knowledge), he, at the same time, wrote the chapter called
Atthasâlinî, on the Dhammasaṅgani (one of the commentaries on the Abhidhamma).

'Revata Thera then observing that he was desirous of
undertaking the compilation of a general commentary
on the Piṭakattaya, thus addressed him: "The text
alone of the Piṭakattaya has been preserved in this land,
the Atthakathâ are not extant here, nor is there any
version to be found of the schisms (vâda) complete. The
Sinhalese Atthakathâ are genuine. They were composed in the Sinhalese language by the inspired and profoundly wise Mahinda, who had previously consulted the
discourses (kathâmagga) of Buddha, authenticated at the
three convocations, and the dissertations and arguments of
Sâriputta and others, and they are extant among the Sinhalese. Preparing for this, and studying the same, translate
them according to the rules of the grammar of the Mâga-
dhas. It will be an act conducive to the welfare of the
whole world."

'Having been thus advised, this eminently wise personage
rejoicing therein, departed from thence, and visited this
island in the reign of this monarch (i. e. Mahânâma, 410–
432). On reaching the Mahâvihâra (at Anurâdhapura), he
entered the Mahâpadhâna hall, the most splendid of the
apartments in the vihâra, and listened to the Sinhalese
Atthakathâ, and the Theravâda, from the beginning to the
end, propounded by the Thera Saṅghapâla; and became
thoroughly convinced that they conveyed the true meaning
of the doctrines of the Lord of Dhamma. Thereupon
paying reverential respect to the priesthood, he thus peti-
tioned: "I am desirous of translating the Atthakathâ;
give me access to all your books." The priesthood, for the
purpose of testing his qualifications, gave only two gâthâs,
saying, "Hence prove thy qualification; having satisfied
ourselves on this point, we will then let thee have all our
books." From these (taking these gâthâ for his text), and

consulting the Piṭakattaya, together with the Aṭṭhakathâ, and condensing them into an abridged form, he composed the work called the Visuddhimagga. Thereupon, having assembled the priesthood, who had acquired a thorough knowledge of the doctrines of Buddha, at the Bo-tree, he commenced to read out the work he had composed. The devatâs, in order that they might make his (Buddhaghosa's) gifts of wisdom celebrated among men, rendered that book invisible. He, however, for a second and third time re-composed it. When he was in the act of producing his book for the third time, for the purpose of propounding it, the devatâs restored the other two copies also. The assembled priests then read out the three books simultaneously. In those three versions there was no variation whatever from the orthodox Theravâdas in passages, in words, or in syllables. Thereupon, the priesthood rejoicing, again and again fervently shouted forth, saying, "Most assuredly this is Metteya (Buddha) himself," and made over to him the books in which the Piṭakattaya were recorded, together with the Aṭṭhakathâ. Taking up his residence in the secluded Ganthâkara-vihâra (at Anurâdhapura), he translated, according to the grammatical rules of the Mâga-dhas, which is the root of all languages, the whole of the Sinhalese Aṭṭhakathâ (into Pâli). This proved an achievement of the utmost consequence to all beings, whatever their language.

'All the Theras and Âkâriyas held this compilation in the same estimation as the text (of the Piṭakattaya). There-after, the objects of his mission having been fulfilled, he returned to Gambudîpa, to worship at the Bo-tree (at Uru-velâya, or Uruvilvâ, in Magadha).'

Here[1] we have a simple account of Buddhaghosa[2] and

[1] Mahâvaṃsa, p. 250, translated by Turnour.

[2] The Burmese entertain the highest respect for Buddhaghosa. Bishop Bigandet, in his Life or Legend of Gaudama (Rangoon, 1866), writes: ' It is perhaps as well to mention here an epoch which has been, at all times, famous in the history of Budhism in Burma. I allude to the voyage which a Religious of Thaton, named Budhagosa, made to Ceylon, in the year of religion 943 = 400 A.D. The object of this voyage was to procure a copy of the scriptures. He succeeded in his undertaking. He made use of the Burmese, or rather Talaing

his literary labours written by a man, himself a priest, and who may well have known Buddhaghosa during his stay in Ceylon. It is true that the statement of his writing the same book three times over without a single various reading, partakes a little of the miraculous; but we find similar legends mixed up with accounts of translations of other sacred books, and we cannot contend that writers who believed in such legends are therefore altogether unworthy to be believed as historical witnesses.

But although the date which we can assign to Buddhaghosa's translation of the commentaries on the Pâli Tipiṭaka proves the existence of that canon, not only for the beginning of the fifth century of our era, but likewise, though it may be, with less stringency, for the first century before our era, the time of Vaṭṭagâmani, the question whether Buddhaghosa was merely a compiler and translator of old commentaries, and more particularly of the commentaries brought to Ceylon by Mahinda (241 B.C.), or whether he added anything of his own [1], requires to be more carefully examined. The Buddhists themselves have no difficulty on that point. They consider the Aṭṭhakathâs or commentaries as old as the canon itself. To us, such a supposition seems improbable, yet it has never been proved to be impossible. The Mahâvaṃsa tells us that Mahinda, the son of Asoka, who had become a priest, learnt the whole of the Buddhist canon, as it then was, in three years (p. 37) [2]; and that at the end of the Third Council he was despatched to Ceylon, in order to establish there the religion of Buddha (p. 71). The king of Ceylon, Devânampiya Tissa, was converted, and Buddhism soon became the dominant

characters, in transcribing the manuscripts, which were written with the characters of Magatha. The Burmans lay much stress upon that voyage, and always carefully note down the year it took place. In fact, it is to Budhagosa that the people living on the shores of the Gulf of Martaban owe the possession of the Budhist scriptures. From Thaton, the collection made by Budhagosa was transferred to Pagan, six hundred and fifty years after it had been imported from Ceylon.' See ibid. p. 392.

[1] He had written the Ñânodaya, and the Aṭṭhasâlinî, a commentary on the Dhamma-sangaṇi, before he went to Ceylon. Cf. Mahâvaṃsa, p. 251.

[2] He learnt the five Nikâyas, and the seven sections (of the Abhidhamma); the two Vibhaṅgas of the Vinaya, the Parivâra and the Khandhaka. See Dîpavaṃsa VII, 42.

religion of the island. The Tipitaka and the Atthakathâ, such as they had been collected or settled at the Third Council in 242 B.C., were brought to Ceylon by Mahinda, who promulgated them orally, the Tipitaka in Pâli, the Atthakathâ in Sinhalese, together with an additional Atthakathâ of his own. It does not follow that Mahinda knew the whole of that enormous literature by heart, for, as he was supported by a number of priests, they may well have divided the different sections among them, following the example of Ânanda and Upâli at the First Council. The same applies to their disciples also. But the fact of their transmitting the sacred literature by oral tradition[1] was evidently quite familiar to the author of the Mahâvamsa. For when he comes to describe the reign of Vattagâmani (88–76 B.C.) he simply says : ʻ The profoundly wise priests had heretofore orally perpetuated the Pâli Pitakattaya and its Atthakathâ (commentaries). At this period these priests, foreseeing the perdition of the people (from the perversions of the true doctrines), assembled; and in order that the religion might endure for ages, wrote the same in books.ʼ No valid objection has yet been advanced to our accepting Buddhaghosa's Atthakathâs as a translation and new re-daction of the Atthakathâs which were reduced to writing under Vattagâmani[2], and these again as a translation of the old Atthakathâs brought to Ceylon by Mahinda[3]. There is prima facie evidence in favour of the truth of historical events vouched for by such works as the Dîpavamsa and the Mahâvamsa so far back at least as Mahinda, because we know that historical events were recorded in the monasteries of Ceylon long before Mahânâma's time. Beyond Mahinda we move in legendary history, and must be ready to surrender every name and every date as soon as rebutting evidence has been produced, but not till then.

I cannot, therefore, see any reason why we should not treat the verses of the Dhammapada, if not as the utter-ances of Buddha, at least as what were believed by the

---

[1] On the importance of oral tradition in the history of Sanskrit literature see the writer's Ancient Sanskrit Literature, 1859, pp. 497–524.

[2] Mahâvamsa, p. 207; Dîpavamsa XX, 20. [3] Mahâvamsa, p. 251.

members of the Council under Asoka, in 242 B.C., to have been the utterances of the founder of their religion; nor can I see that Professor Minayeff has shaken the date of Buddhaghosa and the general credibility of the Ceylonese tradition, that he was the translator and editor of commentaries which had existed in the island for many centuries, whether from the time of Vaṭṭagâmani or from the time of Mahinda.

DATE OF THE BUDDHIST CANON.

We now return to the question of the date of the Buddhist canon, which, as yet, we have only traced back to the first century before Christ, when it was reduced to writing in Ceylon under King Vaṭṭagâmani. The question is, how far beyond that date we may trace its existence in a collected form, or in the form of the three Piṭakas or baskets. There may be, and we shall see that there is, some doubt as to the age of certain works, now incorporated in the Tipiṭaka. We are told, for instance, that some doubt attached to the canonicity of the Kariyâ-piṭaka, the Apadâna, and the Buddhavaṃsa[1], and there is another book of the Abhidhammapiṭaka, the Kathâvatthu, which was reported to be the work of Tissa Moggaliputta, the president of the Third Council. Childers, s. v., stated that it was composed by the apostle Moggaliputtatissa, and delivered by him at the Third Mahâsaṅgîti. The same scholar, however, withdrew this opinion on p. 507 of his valuable Dictionary, where he says: ‘It is a source of great regret to me that in my article on Kathâvatthuppakaraṇam I inadvertently followed James D’Alwis in the stupendous blunder of his assertion that the Kathâvatthu was added by Moggaliputtatissa’ at the Third Convocation. The Kathâvatthu is one of the Abhidhamma books, mentioned by Buddhaghosa as having been rehearsed at the First Convocation, immediately after Gotama’s death; and the passage in Mahâvaṃsa upon which D’Alwis rests his assertion is as follows, Kathâvatthuppakararaṇam paravâdappamaddanaṃ abhâsi Tissatthero ka tasmiṃ saṅgîtimaṇḍale, which simply means ‘in that Convocation-assem-

---

[1] See Childers, s. v. Nikâya.

bly the Thera Tissa also recited (Buddha's) heresy-crushing Kathâvatthuppakara*n*a.'

This mistake, for I quite agree with Childers that it was a mistake, becomes however less stupendous than at first sight it would appear, when we read the account given in the Dîpava*m*sa. Here the impression is easily conveyed that Moggaliputta was the author of the Kathâvatthu, and that he recited it for the first time at the Third Council. 'Wise Moggaliputta,' we read [1], 'the destroyer of the schismatic doctrines, firmly established the Theravâda, and held the Third Council. Having destroyed the different (heretical) doctrines, and subdued many shameless people, and restored splendour to the (true) faith, he proclaimed (pakâsayi) (the treatise called) Kathâvatthu.' And again: 'They all were sectarians [2], opposed to the Theravâda; and in order to annihilate them and to make his own doctrine resplendent, the Thera set forth (desesi) the treatise belonging to the Abhidhamma, which is called Kathâvatthu [3].'

At present, however, we are not concerned with these smaller questions. We treat the canon as a whole, divided into three parts, and containing the books which still exist in MSS., and we want to find out at what time such a collection was made. The following is a short abstract of the Tipi*t*aka, chiefly taken from Childers' Pâli Dictionary:

I. Vinaya-pi*t*aka.

1. Vibhaṅga [4].
     Vol. I, beginning with Pârâ*g*ika, or sins involving expulsion.
     Vol. II, beginning with Pâ*k*ittiya, or sins involving penance.
2. Khandhaka.
     Vol. I, Mahâvagga, the large section.
     Vol. II, *K*ullavagga, the small section.
3. Parivârapâ*th*a, an appendix and later resumé (25 chapters). See p. xiii, n. 4; p. xxiv, n. 2.

---

[1] Dîpava*m*sa VII, 40.   [2] Dîpava*m*sa VII, 55.
[3] Dr. Oldenberg, in his Introduction to the Vinaya-pi*t*aka, p. xxxii.
[4] Oldenberg, Vinaya-pi*t*aka I, p. xvi, treats it as an extended reading of the Pâtimokkha.

II. Sutta-pi*t*aka.

1. Dîgha-nikâya, collection of long suttas (34 suttas)[1].
2. Ma*ggh*ima-nikâya, collection of middle suttas (152 suttas).
3. Sa*m*yutta-nikâya, collection of joined suttas.
4. Anguttara-nikâya[2], miscellaneous suttas, in divisions the length of which increases by one.
5. Khuddaka-nikâya[3], the collection of short suttas, consisting of—
   1. Khuddakapâ*th*a, the small texts[4].
   2. Dhammapada, law verses (423)[5].
   3. Udâna, praise (82 suttas).
   4. Itivuttaka, stories referring to sayings of Buddha.
   5. Suttanipâta, 70 suttas[6].
   6. Vimânavatthu, stories of Vimânas, celestial palaces.
   7. Petavatthu, stories of Pretas, departed spirits.
   8. Theragâthâ, stanzas of monks.
   9. Therîgâthâ, stanzas of nuns.
   10. *G*âtaka, former births (550 tales)[7].
   11. Niddesa, explanations of certain suttas by Sâriputta.

---

[1] The Mahâparinibbâna-sutta, ed. by Childers, Journal of the Royal Asiatic Society, translated with other Suttas by Rhys Davids (S. B. E. vol. xi). Sept Suttas Palis, par Grimblot, Paris, 1876.

[2] The first four are sometimes called the Four Nikâyas, the five together the Five Nikâyas. They represent the Dharma, as settled at the First and Second Councils, described in the *K*ullavagga (Oldenberg, I, p. xi).

[3] Sometimes Khuddaka-nikâya stands for the whole Vinaya and Abhidhamma-pi*t*aka, with the fifteen divisions here given of Khuddaka-nikâya. In the commentary on the Brahma*g*âla-sutta it is said that the Dîghanikâya professors rehearsed the text of the *G*âtaka, Mahâ and *K*ulla Niddesa, Pa*t*isambhidâmagga, Suttanipâta, Dhammapada, Udâna, Itivuttaka, Vimâna, and Petavatthu, Thera and Therî Gâthâ, and called it Khuddakagantha, and made it a canonical text, forming part of the Abhidhamma; while the Ma*ggh*imanikâya professors assert that, with the addition of the *K*ariyâpi*t*aka, Apadâna, and Buddhava*m*sa, the whole of this Khuddakagantha was included in the Suttapi*t*aka. See Childers, s. v. Nikâya. See also p. x.

[4] Published by Childers, Journal of the Royal Asiatic Society, 1869.

[5] Published by Fausböll, 1855.

[6] Thirty translated by Sir Coomâra Swâmy; the whole by Fausböll, in Sacred Books of the East, vol. x.

[7] Published by Fausböll, translated by Rhys Davids.

12. Pa*t*isambhidâmagga, the road of discrimination, and intuitive insight.

13. Apadâna [1], legends.

14. Buddhava*m*sa [1], story of twenty-four preceding Bud-dhas and of Gotama.

15. *K*ariyâpi*t*aka [1], basket of conduct, Buddha's meritorious actions [2].

III. Abhidhamma-pi*t*aka.

1. Dhammasa*n*ga*n*i, numeration of conditions of life [3].
2. Vibha*n*ga, disquisitions (18).
3. Kathâvatthupakara*n*a, book of subjects for discussion (1000 suttas).
4. Puggalapa*ññ*atti or pa*nn*atti, declaration on puggala, or personality.
5. Dhâtukathâ, account of dhâtus or elements.
6. Yamaka, pairs (ten divisions).
7. Pa*tth*ânapakara*n*a, book of causes.

Taking this collection as a whole we may lay it down as self-evident that the canon, in its collected form, cannot be older than any of the events related therein.

There are two important facts for determining the age of the Pâli canon, which, as Dr. Oldenberg [4] has been the first to show, should take precedence of all other arguments, viz.

1. That in the Tipi*t*aka, as we now have it, no mention is made of the so-called Third Council, which took place at Pâ*t*aliputta, under King Asoka, about 242 B.C.

2. That in the Tipi*t*aka, as we now have it, the First Council of Râ*g*agaha (477 B.C.) and the Second Council of Vesâlî (377 B.C.) are both mentioned.

From these two facts it may safely be concluded that the Buddhist canon, as handed down to us, was finally closed

---

[1] Buddhaghosa does not say whether these were recited at the First Council.

[2] Partly translated by Gogerly, Journal of the Asiatic Society of Ceylon, 1852.

[3] Cf. Gogerly, Journal of the Asiatic Society of Ceylon. 1848, p. 7.

[4] See Oldenberg's Vinaya-pi*t*aka, Introduction, p. xxv. The kings Ag*â*tasatru (485-453 B.C.), Udâyin (453-437 B.C.), and Mu*n*da (437-429 B.C.) are all mentioned in the Tipi*t*aka. See Oldenberg, Zeitschrift der D. M. G., XXXIV, pp. 752, 753.

after the Second and before, or possibly at, the Third Council. Nay, the fact that the description of the two Councils stands at the very end of the *K*ullavagga may be taken, as Dr. Oldenberg remarks, as an indication that it was one of the latest literary contributions which obtained canonical authority, while the great bulk of the canon may probably claim a date anterior to the Second Council.

This fact, namely, that the collection of the canon, as a whole, must have preceded the Second Council rests on an argument which does great credit to the ingenuity of Dr. Oldenberg. The Second Council was 'convoked to consider the ten deviations[1] from the strict discipline of the earliest times. That discipline had been laid down first in the Pâtimokkha rules, then in the commentary now included in the Vibhaṅga, lastly in the Mahâvagga and *K*ullavagga. The rules as to what was allowed or forbidden to a Bhikkhu were most minute[2], and they were so firmly established that no one could have ventured either to take away or to add anything to them as they stood in the sacred code. In that code itself a distinction is made between the offences which were from the first visited with punishment (pârâ*g*ika and pâ*k*ittiya) and those misdemeanours and crimes which were put down as punishable at a later time (dukka*t*a and thulla*kk*aya). With these classes the code was considered as closed, and if any doubt arose as to the criminality of certain acts, it could be settled at once by an appeal to the Vinaya-pi*t*aka. Now it so happens that, with one exception, the ten deviations that had to be considered at the Second Council, are not provided for in the Vinaya-pi*t*aka ; and I quite agree with Dr. Oldenberg's argument that, if they had been mentioned in the Vinaya-pi*t*aka, the Second Council would have been objectless. A mere appeal to chapter and verse in the existing Pi*t*aka would then have silenced all dissent. On the other side, if it had been possible to add anything to the canon, as it then existed, the ten, or nine, deviations might have been con-

---

[1] Oldenberg, Introduction, p. xxix.   [2] Oldenberg, loc. cit. p. xx.

demned by a few additional paragraphs of the canon, without convoking a new Council.

I think we may be nearly certain, therefore, that we possess the principal portion of the Vinaya-pitaka as it existed before the Council of Vesâlî.

So far I quite agree with Dr. Oldenberg. But if he proceeds to argue[1] that certain portions of the canon must have been finally settled before even the First Council took place, or was believed to have taken place, I do not think his arguments conclusive. He contends that in the Parinibbâna-sutta, which tells of the last days of Buddha's life, of his death, the cremation of his body, and the distribution of his relics, and of Subhadda's revolt, it would have been impossible to leave out all mention of the First Council, if that Council had then been known. It is true, no doubt, that Subhadda's disloyalty was the chief cause of the First Council, but there was no necessity to mention that Council. On the contrary, it seems to me that the unity of the Parinibbâna-sutta would have been broken if, besides telling of the last days of Buddha, it had also given a full description of the Council. The very title, the Sutta of the Great Decease, would have become inappropriate, if so important a subject as the first Sangîti had been mixed up with it. However, how little we may trust to such general arguments, is best shown by the fact that in some very early Chinese renderings of the Hînayâna text of the Mahâparinibbâna-sutta the story is actually carried on to the First Council, two (Nos. 552 and 119) mentioning the rehearsal under Kasyapa, while the third (No. 118) simply states that the Tipitaka was then collected[2].

---

[1] Loc. cit. pp. xxvi–xxviii.

[2] There are several Chinese translations of Sûtras on the subject of the Mahâparinirvâna. Three belong to the Mahâyâna school: 1. Mahâparinirvâna-sûtra, translated by Dharmaraksha, about 414–423 A. D.; afterwards revised, 424–453 (Nos. 113, 114). 2. Translation by Fa-hian and Buddhabhadra, about 415 A.D.; less complete (No. 120). 3. Translation (vaipulya) by Dharmaraksha I, i.e. Ku Fa-hu, about 261–308 A.D. (No. 116). Three belong to the Hînayâna school: 1. Mahâparinirvâna-sûtra, translated by Po-fa-tsu, about 290–306 A.D. (No. 552). 2. Translation under the Eastern Tsin dynasty, 317–420 A.D. (No. 119). 3. Translation by Fa-hian, about 415 A.D. (No. 118).

We must be satisfied therefore, so far as I can see at present, with fixing the date, and the latest date, of a Buddhist canon at the time of the Second Council, 377 B.C. That some works were added later, we know; that many of the treatises included in the canon existed before that Council, can hardly be doubted. The second chapter of the Dhammapada, for instance, is called the Appamâda-vagga, and if the Mahâvamsa (p. 25) tells us that at the time when Asoka was converted by Nigrodha, that Buddhist priest explained to him the Appamâda-vagga, we can hardly doubt that there existed then a collection (vagga) of verses on Appamâda, such as we now possess in the Dhammapada and in the Samyutta-nikâya [1].

With regard to the Vinaya, I should even feel inclined to admit, with Dr. Oldenberg, that it must have existed in a more or less settled form before that time. What I doubt is whether such terms as Pitaka, basket, or Tipitaka, the three baskets, i. e. the canon, existed at that early time. They have not been met with, as yet, in any of the canonical books; and if the Dîpavamsa (IV, 32) uses the word 'Tipitaka,' when describing the First Council, this is due to its transferring new terms to older times. If Dr. Oldenberg speaks of a Dvi-pitaka [2] as the name of the canon before the third basket, that of the Abhidhamma, was admitted, this seems to me an impossible name, because at the time when the Abhidhamma was not yet recognised as a third part of the canon, the word pitaka had probably no existence as a technical term [3].

We must always, I think, distinguish between the three portions of the canon, called the basket of the Suttas, the

[1] Feer, Revue Critique, 1870, No. 24, p. 377.   [2] Introduction, pp. x, xii.

[3] Dr. Oldenberg informs me that pitaka occurs in the Kankîsuttanta in the Magghima Nikâya (Turnour's MS., fol. the), but applied to the Veda. He also refers to the tipitakâkâryas mentioned in the Western Cave inscriptions as compared with the Pañkanekâyâka in the square Asoka character inscriptions (Cunningham, Bharhut, pl. lvi, No. 52). In the Sûtrakrid-anga of the Gainas, too, the term pidagam occurs (MS. Berol. fol. 77 a). He admits, however, that pitaka or tipitaka, as the technical name of the Buddhist canon, has not yet been met with in that canon itself, and defends Dvipitaka only as a convenient term.

basket of Vinaya, and the basket of Abhidhamma, and
the three subjects of Dhamma (sutta), Vinaya, and Abhidhamma, treated in these baskets. The subjects existed
and were taught long before the three baskets were definitely arranged. Dhamma had originally a much wider
meaning than Sutta-pi/aka. It often means the whole
teaching of Buddha; and even when it refers more particularly to the Sutta-pi/aka, we know that the Dhamma
there taught deals largely with Vinaya and Abhidhamma
doctrines. Even the fact that at the First Council, according to the description given in the *K*ullavagga, the Vinaya
and Dhamma only were rehearsed, though proving the
absence at that time of the Abhidhamma, as a separate
Pi/aka, by no means excludes the subject of the Abhidhamma having been taught under the head of Dhamma.
In the Mahâkaru*n*âpu*nd*arîka-sûtra the doctrine of Buddha
is divided into Dharma and Vinaya; the Abhidharma is
not mentioned. But the same text knows of all the twelve
Dharmaprava*k*anâni [1], the 1. Sûtra; 2. Geya; 3. Vyâka-
ra*n*a; 4. Gâthâ; 5. Udâna; 6. Nidâna; 7. Avadâna; 8.
Itiv*ri*ttaka; 9. *G*âtaka; 10. Vaipulya; 11. Adbhutadharma;
12. Upade*s*a ; some of these being decidedly metaphysical.

To my mind nothing shows so well the historical character
both of the *K*ullavagga and of Buddhaghosa in the Introduction to his commentary on the Dîgha-nikâya, as that the
former, in its account of the First Council, should know
only of the Vinaya, as rehearsed by Upâli, and the Dhamma,
as rehearsed by Ânanda, while the much later Buddhaghosa,
in his account of the First Council [2], divides the Dhamma
into two parts, and states that the second part, the Abhidhamma, was rehearsed after the first part, the Dhamma.
Between the time of the *K*ullavagga and the time of
Buddhaghosa the Abhidhamma must have assumed its
recognised position by the side of Vinaya and Sutta. It
must be left to further researches to determine, if possible,

---

[1] See Academy, August 28, 1880, Division of Buddhist Scriptures.
[2] Oldenberg. Introduction, p. xii ; Turnour, Journal of the Asiatic Society of
Bengal, vi, p. 510 seq.

the time when the name of pi*t*aka was first used, and when
Tipi*t*aka was accepted as the title of the whole canon.

Whenever we see such traces of growth, we feel that we
are on historical ground, and in that sense Dr. Oldenberg's researches into the growth of the Vinaya, previous
to the Second Council, deserve the highest credit. He
shows, in opposition to other scholars, that the earliest
elements of Vinaya must be looked for in the short Pâtimokkha rules, which were afterwards supplemented by
explanations, by glosses and commentaries, and in that
form answered for some time every practical purpose.
Then followed a new generation who, not being satisfied,
as it would seem, with these brief rules and comments,
wished to know the occasion on which these rules had been
originally promulgated. What we now call the Vibhaṅga,
i. e. the first and second divisions of the Vinaya-pi*t*aka, is
a collection of the stories, illustrating the origin of each
rule, of the rules themselves (the Pâtimokkha), and of the
glosses and comments on these rules.

The third and fourth books, the Mahâvagga and *K*ullavagga, are looked upon as possibly of a slightly later date.
They treat, in a similar manner as the Vibhaṅga, on the rules
not included in that collection, and give a general picture
of the outward life of the monks. While the Vibhaṅga deals
chiefly with the original so-called pârâ*g*ika, saṅghâdisesa, and
pâ*k*ittîya offences, the Khandhaka, i. e. the Mahâvagga
and *K*ullavagga, treats of the so-called dukka*t*a and thulla*kk*aya crimes. The arrangement is the same, story, rule,
and comment succeeding each other in regular sequence.

If we follow the guidance of the Vinaya-pi*t*aka, we should
be able to distinguish the following steps in the growth of
Buddhism before the Second Council of Vesâlî :

1. Teaching of Buddha and his disciples (543/477 A. D.
   Buddha's death).
2. Collection of Pâtimokkha rules (first code).
3. Comment and glosses on these rules.
4. Stories in illustration of these rules (vibhaṅga).
5. Mahâvagga and *K*ullavagga (Khandhaka).

6. Council of Vesâlî for the repression of ten abuses (443/377 A.D.)

7. Description of First and Second Councils in *K*ullavagga. The *K*ullavagga ascribes the settlement of the canon to the First Council, and does not even claim a revision of that canon for the Second Council. The Dîpava*m*sa claims a revision of the canon by the 700 Arhats for the Second Council.

CHRONOLOGY.

In order to bring the Council of Vesâlî in connection with the chronology of the world, we must follow the Buddhist historians for another century. One hundred and eighteen years after the Council of Vesâlî they place the anointment of King Asoka, during whose reign a Third Council, under the presidency of Tissa Moggaliputta, took place at Pâ*t*aliputta, the new capital adopted by that king, instead of Râ*g*agaha and Vesâlî. This Council is chiefly known to us through the writings of the southern Buddhists (Dîpava*m*sa, Mahâva*m*sa, and Buddhaghosa), who belong to the school of Moggaliputta (Theravâda or Vibha*gg*avâda), which ruled supreme at Pâ*t*aliputta, while Upagupta, the chief authority of the northern Buddhists, is altogether ignored in the Pâli chronicles.

Now it is well known that Asoka was the grandson of *K*andagutta, and *K*andagutta the contemporary of Alexander the Great. Here we see land, and I may refer to my History of Sanskrit Literature, published in 1859, for the process by which the storm-tossed ship of Indian chronology has been landed in the harbour of real historical chronology. We are told by the monks of the Mahâvihâra in Ceylon that Asoka was crowned, according to their computation, 146 + 18 years before the accession of Du*tth*agâmani, 161 B.C., i.e. 325 B.C.; that between his coronation and his father's death four years had elapsed (329 B.C.); that his father Bindusâra had reigned twenty-eight years [1] (357–329 B.C.), and Bindusâra's father, *K*an-

---

[1] Mahâva*m*sa, p. 21.

dagutta, twenty-four years (381–357). As we know that
*K*andagutta, whom the Ceylonese place 381–357 B.C., was
king of India after Alexander's conquest, it follows that
Ceylonese chronology is wrong by more than half a
century. For reasons stated in my History of Sanskrit
Literature, I fix the exact fault in Ceylonese chronology
as sixty-six years, assigning to *K*andagutta the dates
315–291, instead of 381–357. This gives us 291–263 for
Bindusâra, 259 for Asoka's abhisheka; 259 + 118 = 377
for the Council of Vesâlî, and 377 + 100 = 477 for Buddha's
death, instead of 543 B.C.[1]

These dates are, of course, approximate only, and they
depend on one or two points on which people may differ.
But, with that reservation, I see no ground whatever for
modifying the chronological system which I put forward
more than twenty years ago. Professor Westergaard and
Professor Kern, who have since suggested different dates
for the death of Buddha, do not really differ from me in
principle, but only in their choice of one or the other alter-
native, which I readily admit as possible, but not as more
certain than my own. Professor Westergaard[2], for instance,
fixes Buddha's death at 368 (370), instead of 477. This
seems a wide difference, but it is so in appearance only.

Following Justinus, who says that Sandrokyptos[3] had
conquered the empire of India at the time when Seleucus
laid the foundations of his own greatness, I had accepted
315[4], half-way between the murder of Porus and the
taking of Babylon by Seleucus, as the probable beginning

---

[1] According to Bigandet, Life of Gaudama, p. 361, the era of Buddha's death
was introduced by Agâtasatru, at the conclusion of the First Council, and
began in the year 146 of the older Eetzana era (p. 12). See, however, Rhys
Davids, Num. Orient. vi, p. 38. In the Kâra*n*da-vyûha, p. 96, a date is given
as 300 after the Nirvâ*n*a, ' trit*i*ye varshasate gate mama parinirv*ri*tasya.' In the
Asoka-avadâna we read, mama nirv*ri*tim ârabhya satavarshagata Upagupto
nâma bhikshur utpatsyati.

[2] Über Buddha's Todesjahr (1860), 1862.

[3] The Greek name Sandrokyptus shows that the Pâli corruption *K*andagutta
was not yet the recognised name of the king.

[4] Mr. Rhys Davids accepts 315 B.C. as the date when, after the murder of
king Nanda, *K*andragupta stept into the vacant throne, though he had begun
to count his reign seven or eight years before. Buddhism, p. 220.

of *K*andragupta's reign. Westergaard prefers 320 as a more likely date for *K*andragupta, and therefore places the death of the last Nanda and the beginning of A*s*oka's royal pretensions 268. Here there is a difference between him and me of five years, which depends chiefly on the view we take as to the time when Seleucus really laid what Justinus calls the foundation of his future greatness. Secondly, Westergaard actually adopts the idea, at which I only hinted as possible, that the southern Buddhists made two A*s*okas out of one, and two Councils out of one. Trusting in the tradition that 118 years elapsed between Buddha's death and the Council under A*s*oka (at Pâ*t*aliputra), and that the Council took place in the king's tenth year (as was the case with the imaginary Kâlâ*s*oka's Council), he gets 268—10=258 as the date of the Council, and 368 or 370 as the date of Buddha's death [1].

The two points on which Westergaard differs from me, seem to me questions which should be kept before our mind in dealing with early Buddhist history, but which, for the present at least, admit of no definite solution.

The same remark seems to me to apply to the calculations of another eminent Sanskrit scholar, Professor Kern [2]. He lays great stress on the general untrustworthiness of Indian chronology, and I am the last to differ from him on that point. He then places the beginning of *K*andragupta's reign in 322 B.C. Allowing twenty-four years to him and twenty-eight to his son Bindusâra, he places the beginning of A*s*oka's reign in 270. A*s*oka's inscriptions would fall about 258. As A*s*oka reigned thirty-six or thirty-seven years, his death would fall in 234 or 233 B.C. Like Westergaard, Professor Kern too eliminates Kâlâ*s*oka, as a kind of chronological A*s*oka, and the Council of Vai*s*âlî, and therefore places Buddha's death, according to the northern tradition, 100 or 110 years before Dharmâ*s*oka, i.e. 270+100 or +110=370 or 380 [3]; while, according to the southern

---

[1] Westergaard, loc. cit. p. 128.
[2] Jaartelling der Zuidelijke Buddhisten, 1873.
[3] See Professor Kern's remark in Indian Antiquary, 1874, p. 79.

tradition, that 118 years elapsed between Asoka's accession and Buddha's death, the Ceylonese monks would seem originally to have retained $270 + 118^1 = 388$ B.C. as Buddha's Nirvâna, a date which, as Professor Kern holds, happens to coincide with the date assigned to the death of Mahâvîra, the founder of the Gaina religion.

Here we see again that the moot point is the beginning of Kandragupta's reign in accordance with the information supplied by Greek historians. Professor Kern places it in 322, Westergaard in 320, I myself in 315. That difference once granted, Dr. Kern's reasoning is the same as my own. According to the traditions which we follow, Buddha's death took place 100, 110, 118, or 228 years before Asoka. Hence Professor Westergaard arrives at 368 or 370 B.C. Professor Kern at 370 (380) or 388 B.C., I myself at 477 B.C. Every one of these dates is liable to certain objections, and if I prefer my own date, 477 B.C., it is simply because it seems to me liable to neither more nor less reservations than those of Professor Westergaard and Professor Kern, and because, so long as we always remember the grounds of our differences, namely, the beginning of Kandragupta's reign, and the additional century, every one of these dates furnishes a good hypothesis to work on, until we can arrive at greater certainty in the ancient chronology of India.

To my mind all dates beyond Kandragupta are as yet purely tentative, resting far more on a chronological theory than on actual tradition; and though I do not doubt the historical character of the Council of Vaisâlî, I look upon the date assigned to it, on the authority of the Dîpavamsa and Mahâvamsa, as, for the present, hypothetical only.

---

[1] When Professor Kern states that the Mahâvamsa (p. 22) places the Third Council 218 years after Buddha's death, this is not so. Asoka's abhisheka takes place in that year. The prophecy that a calamity would befall their religion, 118 years after the Second Council (Mahâvamsa, p. 28), does not refer to the Council, but to Kandâsoka's accession, $477 - 218 = 259$ B. C.

B.C.
557. Buddha born.
552. Bimbisâra born.
537–485. Bimbisâra, 5 years younger than Buddha, was
15 when crowned, 30 or 31 when he met Buddha in 522.
485–453. Agâta*s*atru (4 × 8 years).
477. Buddha's death (485—8=477).
477. COUNCIL AT RÂGAGR*I*HA under Kâ*s*yapa, Ânanda,
and Upâli.
453–437. Udâyibhadra (2 × 8 years).
437–429. { Anuruddhaka (8 years).
          { Mu*nd*a (at Pâ*t*aliputra).
429–405. Nâgadâsaka (3 × 8 years).
405–387. *S*i*s*unâga (at Vai*s*âlî).
387–359. Kâlâ*s*oka.
377. COUNCIL AT VAI*s*ÂLÎ, under Ya*s*as and Revata,
a disciple of Ânanda (259+118=377).
359–337. Ten sons of Kâlâ*s*oka (22 years).
337–315. Nine Nandas (22 years); the last, Dhana-
nanda, killed by *K*â*n*akya.
315–291. *K*andragupta (477—162=315; 3 × 8 years)[1].
291–263. Bindusâra.
263–259. A*s*oka, sub-king at Ug*g*ayinî, as pretender—
his brothers killed.
259. A*s*oka anointed at Pâ*t*aliputra (477—218=259).
256. A*s*oka converted by Nigrodha (D.V. VI, 18).
256–253. Building of Vihâras, Sthûpas, &c.
255. Conversion of Tishya (M.V. p. 34).
253. Ordination of Mahendra (born 477—204=273).
251. Tishya and Sumitra die (D.V. VII, 32).
242. COUNCIL AT PÂTALIPUTRA (259—17=242; 477—
236=241), under Tishya Maudgalîputra (477—236=241 ;
D.V. VII, 37).
241. Mahendra to Ceylon.
222. A*s*oka died (259—37=222).
193. Mahendra died (D.V. XVII, 93).
161. Du*tth*agâmani.
88–76. Vattagâmani, canon reduced to writing.
A.D.
400. Dîpava*m*sa.
420. Buddhaghosha, Pâli commentaries.
459–477. Mahâva*m*sa.

---

[1] Westergaard, 320—296; Kern, 322—298.

Though the preceding table, embodying in the main the results at which I arrived in my History of Ancient Sanskrit Literature, still represents what I hold to be true or most probable with respect to Indian chronology, previous to the beginning of our era, yet I suppose I may be expected to say here a few words on the two latest attempts to fix the date of Buddha's death ; the one by Mr. Rhys Davids in the Numismata Orientalia, Part VI, 1877, the other by Dr. Bühler in the Indian Antiquary, 1877 and 1878 [1]. Mr. Rhys Davids, to whom we owe so much for the elucidation of the history of Buddha's religion, accepts Westergaard's date for the beginning of *K*andragupta's reign, 320 B.C., instead of 322 (Kern), 315 (myself); and as he assigns (p. 41) to Bindusâra 25 years instead of 28 (Mahâva*m*sa, p. 21), he arrives at 268 as the year of A*s*oka's coronation [2]. He admits that the argument derived from the mention of the five foreign kings in one of A*s*oka's inscriptions, dated the twelfth year of his reign, is too precarious to enable us to fix the date of A*s*oka's reign more definitely, and though, in a general way, that inscription confirms the date assigned by nearly all scholars to A*s*oka in the middle of the third century B.C., yet there is nothing in it that A*s*oka might not have written in 247 quite as well as in 258-261. What chiefly distinguishes Mr. Rhys Davids' chronology from that of his predecessors is the shortness of the period between A*s*oka's coronation and Buddha's death. On the strength of an examination of the list of kings and the list of the so-called patriarchs, he reduces the traditional 218 years to 140 or 150, and thus arrives at 412 B.C. as the probable beginning of the Buddhist era.

In this, however, I cannot follow him, but have to follow Dr. Bühler. As soon as I saw Dr. Bühler's first essay on the Three New Edicts of A*s*oka, I naturally felt delighted at the unexpected confirmation which he furnished of the date which I had assigned to Buddha's death, 477 B.C. And though I am quite aware of the

---

[1] Three New Edicts of Asoka, Bombay, 1877 ; Second Notice, Bombay, 1878.

[2] Mr. Rhys Davids on p. 50 assigns the 25 years of Bindusâra rightly to the Purâ*n*as, the 28 years to the Ceylon Chronicles.

danger of unexpected confirmations of one's own views, yet, after carefully weighing the objections raised by Mr. Rhys Davids and Professor Pischel against Dr. Bühler's arguments, I cannot think that they have shaken Dr. Bühler's position. I fully admit the difficulties in the phraseology of these inscriptions: but I ask, Who could have written these inscriptions, if not Asoka? And how, if written by Asoka, can the date which they contain mean anything but 256 years after Buddha's Nirvâna? These points, however, have been argued in so masterly a manner by Dr. Bühler in his 'Second Notice,' that I should be afraid of weakening his case by adding anything of my own, and must refer my readers to his 'Second Notice.' Allowing that latitude which, owing to the doubtful readings of MSS., and the constant neglect of odd months, we must allow in the interpretation of Buddhist chronology, Asoka is the only king we know of who could have spoken of a thirty-fourth year since the beginning of his reign and since his conversion to Buddhism. And if he calls that year, say the very last of his reign (222 B.C.), 256 after the departure of the Master, we have a right to say that as early as Asoka's time, Buddha was believed to have died about 477 B.C. Whether the inscriptions have been accurately copied and rightly read is, however, a more serious question, and the doubts raised by Dr. Oldenberg (Mahâvagga, p. xxxviii) make a new collation of the originals absolutely indispensable, before we can definitely accept Dr. Bühler's interpretation.

I cannot share Dr. Bühler's opinion[1] as to the entire worthlessness of the Gaina chronology in confirming the date of Buddha's death. If the Svetâmbara Gainas place the death of Mahâvîra 470 before Vikramâditya, i. e. 56 B.C. +470=526 B.C., and the Digambaras 605, i.e. 78 A.D. deducted from 605=527 B.C., this so far confirms Dr. Bühler's and Dr. Jacobi's brilliant discovery that Mahâvîra was the same as Nigantha Nâtaputta, who died at Pâvâ during Buddha's lifetime[2]. Most likely 527 is too early a date, while another

---

[1] Three Edicts, p. 21; Second Notice, pp. 9, 10.
[2] See Jacobi, Kalpa-sûtra of Bhadrabâhu, and Oldenberg, Zeitschrift der D. M. G., XXXIV, p. 749.

tradition fixing Mahâvîra's death 155 years before *K*andragupta[1], 470 B.C., is too late. Yet they both show that
the distance between A*s*oka (259–222 B.C.), the grandson
of *K*andragupta (315–291 B.C.), and the contemporaries of
Buddha was by the *G*ainas also believed to be one of two
rather than one century.

When I saw that the date of Buddha's death, 477 B.C.,
which in my History of Ancient Sanskrit Literature (1859)
I had myself tried to support by such arguments as were
then accessible, had received so powerful a support by the
discovery of the inscriptions of Sahasrâm, Rûpnâth, and
Bairât, due to General Cunningham, who had himself
always been an advocate of the date 477 B.C., and through
their careful decipherment by Dr. Bühler, I lost no time
in testing that date once more by the Dîpava*m*sa, that
Ceylonese chronicle having lately become accessible through
Dr. Oldenberg's edition and translation[2]. And here I am
able to say that, before having read Dr. Bühler's Second
Notice, I arrived, though by a somewhat different way, at
nearly the same conclusions as those so well worked out by
Dr. Bühler in his restoration of the Episcopal Succession
(therâvali) of the Buddhists, and therefore feel convinced
that, making all such allowances as the case requires, we
know now as much of early Buddhist chronology as could
be known at the time of A*s*oka's Council, 242 B.C.

Taking the date of Buddha's death 477 B.C. for granted,
I found that Upâli, who rehearsed the Vinaya at the First
Council, 477 B.C., had been in orders sixty years in the
twenty-fourth year of A*g*âta*s*atru, i. e. 461 B.C., which was
the sixteenth year A.B. He must therefore[3] have been born
in 541 B.C., and he died 447 B.C., i. e. thirty years A.B., at
the age of 94. This is said to have been the sixth year of
Udâyi, and so it is, 453 − 6 = 447 B.C.

In the year 461 B.C. Dâ*s*aka received orders from Upâli,
who was then 80 years of age; and when Dâ*s*aka had been

[1] Oldenberg, loc. cit. p. 750.
[2] The Dîpava*m*sa, an ancient Buddhist historical record. London, 1879.
[3] Assuming twenty to be the minimum age at which a man could be ordained.

in orders forty-five years (Dîpava*m*sa IV, 41), he ordained
*S*aunaka. This would give us 461—45=416 B.C., while the
tenth year of Nâgadâsa, 429—10, would give us 419 A.D.
Later on the Dîpava*m*sa (V, 78) allows an interval of forty
years between the ordinations of Dâsaka and *S*aunaka,
which would bring the date of *S*aunaka's ordination to 421
B.C., instead of 419 or 416 B.C. Here there is a fault which
must be noted. Dâsaka died 461—64=397 A.D., which is
called the eighth year of *S*i*s*unâga, and so it is, 405—8=
397 A.D.
When *S*aunaka had been in orders forty years, i. e.
416—40=376, Kâlâ*s*oka is said to have reigned a little
over ten years, i. e. 387—11=376 A.D., and in that year
*S*aunaka ordained Siggava. He died 416—66=350 A.D.,
which is called the sixth year of the Ten, while in reality
it is the ninth, 359—6=353 A.D. If, however, we take 419
as the year of *S*aunaka's ordination, his death would fall
419—66=353 B.C.
Siggava, when he had been in orders sixty-four years,
ordained Tishya Maudgalîputra. This date 376—64=312
B.C. is called more than two years after *K*andragupta's
accession, and so it very nearly is, 315—2=313.
Siggava died when he had been in orders seventy-six
years, i. e. 376—76=300 A.D. This year is called the
fourteenth year of *K*andragupta, which it very nearly is,
315—14=301.
When Tishya had been in orders sixty[1] years, he ordained Mahendra, 312—60=252 B.C. This is called six
years after A*s*oka's coronation, 259—6=253, and so it very
nearly is. He died 312—80=232 B.C., which is called the
twenty-sixth year of A*s*oka, and so it very nearly is.

---

[1] I take 60 (80), as given in Dîpava*m*sa V, 95, 107, instead of 66 (86), as
given in Dîpava*m*sa V, 94.

BUDDHIST PATRIARCHS.

	Birth.	Ordination.	Ordination of successor.	Death.	Age.	Patriarchate.
Upâli	(Generally 20 years before ordination.)	527 (60)	461	447	94	30
Dâsaka		461	416 ⎱ 419 ⎰ 421	397	84	50
		45 ⎱ 42 ⎰ 40				
Saunaka	„	416 ⎱ 419 ⎰ 421 (40)	376 ⎱ 379 ⎰ 381	350 353	86	44 (47)
Siggava	„	376½ (64)	312½	300½	96	50 (52)
Tishya	„	312½ (60)	253	233	100	68
Mahendra	273	253	„	193	80	40

282 (284)

If we test the dates of this table by the length of time assigned to each patriarchate, we find that Upâli ruled thirty years, from Buddha's death, 477 to 447; Dâsaka fifty years. To Saunaka forty-four years are assigned, instead of forty-seven, owing to a fault pointed out before; and to Siggava fifty-two years, or fifty-five [1] instead of fifty. Tishya's patriarchate is said to have lasted sixty-eight years, which agrees with previous statements.

Lastly, the years of the death of the six patriarchs, as fixed according to the reigns of the kings of Magadha, agree extremely well.

Upâli died in the sixth year of Udâyi, i.e.453—6=447 B.C.

Dâsaka died in the eighth year of Sisunâga, i.e. 405—8= 397 B.C.

Saunaka died in the sixth year of the Ten, i.e. 359—6= 353 B.C., showing again the difference of three years.

---

[1] The combined patriarchates of Saunaka and Siggava are given as 99 by the Dîpavamsa.

Siggava died in the fourteenth year of *K*andragupta, i. e.
315—14=301 B.C.

Tishya died in the twenty-sixth or twenty-seventh year
of A*s*oka, i. e. 259—27=233 B.C.

This general and more than general agreement between
dates taken from the history of the kings and the history
of the patriarchs leaves on my mind a decided impression
of a tradition which, though not strictly historical, in our
sense of the word, represents at all events the result of such
enquiries as could be made into the past ages of Buddhism
at the time of A*s*oka. There are difficulties in that tradition
which would certainly have been avoided, if the whole
chronology had been simply made up: but there is no
doubt a certain method too perceptible throughout, which
warns us that we must not mistake a smooth chronology
for solid history.

THE TITLE OF DHAMMAPADA.

The title of Dhammapada has been interpreted in various
ways. It is an ambiguous word, and has been accepted as
such by the Buddhists themselves. Dhamma has many
meanings. Under one aspect it means religion, particularly the religion taught by Buddha, the law which every
Buddhist should accept and observe. Under another aspect
dhamma is virtue, or the realisation of the law.

Pada also has many meanings. In the Abhidhâna-
padîpikâ it is explained by place, protection, Nirvâ*n*a, cause,
word, thing, portion, foot, footstep.

Hence dhammapada may mean 'footstep of religion,'
and thus the title was first rendered by Gogerly, only that
he used the plural instead of the singular, and called it 'The
Footsteps of Religion,' while Spence Hardy still more freely
called it 'The Paths of Religion.' It may be quite true, as
pointed out by Childers, that pada by itself never means
path. But it means footstep, and the footstep towards
a thing is much the same as what we call the path to a
thing. Thus we read, verse 21, 'appamâdo amatapadam,'
earnestness is the step, i.e. the path that leads to immor-

.

tality. Again, 'pamâdo ma*kk*uno padam' can hardly mean
anything but that thoughtlessness is the path of death, is
the path that leads to death. The commentator, too,
rightly explains it here by amatasya adhigamupâya, the
means of obtaining immortality, i. e. Nirvâ*n*a, or simply by
upâyo, and even by maggo, the way. If we compare verses
92 and 93 of our text, and verses 254 and 255, we see that
pada is used synonymously with gati, going. In the
same manner dhammapada would mean the footstep or
the footpath of virtue, i. e. the path that leads to virtue, and
supply a very appropriate title for a collection of moral
precepts. In verses 44 and 45 'path of virtue' seems to be
the most appropriate meaning for dhammapada [1], and it is
hardly possible to assign any other meaning to it in the
following verse (*K*undasutta, v. 6):

> Yo dhammapade sudesite
> Magge *g*îvati sa*ññ*ato satimâ,
> Anava*gg*a-padâni sevamâno
> Tatîyam bhikkhum âhu magga*g*îvim,

'He who lives restrained and attentive in the way that has
been well pointed out, in the path of the law, cultivating
blameless words, such a Bhikkhu they call a Magga*g*îvi
(living in the way).'

I therefore think that 'Path of Virtue,' or 'Footstep of
the Law,' was the idea most prominent in the mind of those
who originally framed the title of this collection of verses.
It seems to me that Buddhaghosa also took the same view,
for the verse which D'Alwis [2] quotes from the introduction
of Buddhaghosa's commentary,—

Sampatta-saddhammapado satthâ dhammapada*m* subha*m*
      Desesi,

and which he translates, 'The Teacher who had reached
the very depths (lit. bottom) of Saddhamma, preached this
holy Dhammapada,'—lends itself far better to another
translation, viz. 'The Teacher who had gained a firm

---

[1] Cf. Dhammapada, v. 285, nibbâna*m* sugatena desita*m*.
[2] Buddhist Nirvâ*n*a, p. 62.

footing in the Good Law, showed (preached) the holy Path of the Law.'

Gogerly, again, who may generally be taken as a faithful representative of the tradition of the Buddhists still preserved in Ceylon, translates the title by the ' Footsteps of Religion,' so that there can be little doubt that the priests of that island accept Dhammapada in the sense of 'Vestiges of Religion,' or, from a different point of view, ' The Path of Virtue.'

M. L. Feer[1] takes a slightly different view, and assigning to pada the meaning of foot or base, he translates Dhammapada by Loi fondamentale, or Base de la Religion.

But it cannot be denied that the title of Dhammapada was very soon understood in a different sense also, namely, as ' Sentences of Religion.' Pada means certainly a foot of a verse, a verse, or a line, and dhammapadam actually occurs in the sense of a ' religious sentence.' Thus we read in verse 102, 'Though a man recite a hundred Gâthâs made up of senseless words, one dhammapadam, i. e. one single word or line of the law, is better, which if a man hears, he becomes quiet.' But here we see at once the difficulty of translating the title of ' dhammapadam' by 'religious sentences.' Dhammapadam means one law verse, or wise saw, not many. Professor Fausböll, who in his excellent edition of the Dhammapada translated that title by ' a collection of verses on religion,' appeals to such passages as verses 44 and 102 in support of his interpretation. But in verse 42 dhammapadam sudesitam, even if it does not mean the path of the law, could never mean 'versus legis bene enarratos,' but only versum legis bene enarratum, as Dr. Fausböll himself renders ekam dhammapadam, in verse 102, by unus legis versus. Buddhaghosa, too, when he speaks of many law verses uses the plural, for instance[2], ' Be it known that the Gâthâ consists of the Dhammapadânî, Theragâthâ, Therîgâthâ, and those unmixed (detached) Gâthâ not comprehended in any of the above-named Suttânta.'

[1] Revue Critique, 1870, p. 378.   [2] D'Alwis, Pâli Grammar, p. 61.

The only way in which Dhammapada could be defended
in the sense of 'Collection of Verses of the Law,' would be
if we took it for an aggregate compound. But such aggregate compounds, in Sanskrit at least, are possible with
numerals only; for instance, tribhuvanam, the three
worlds; *k*aturyugam, the four ages[1]. It might therefore
be possible in Pâli, too, to form such compounds as da*s*a-
padam, a collection of ten padas, a work consisting of ten
padas, a decamerone, but it would in no wise follow that
we could in that language attempt such a compound as
Dhammapadam, in order to express a collection of law
verses[2]. Mr. Beal[3] informs us that the Chinese seem to
have taken Dhammapada in the sense of 'stanzas of law,'
'law texts,' or 'scripture texts.'

It should be remembered, also, that the idea of representing life, and particularly the life of the faithful, as a
path of duty or virtue leading to deliverance, (in Sanskrit
dharmapatha,) is very familiar to Buddhists. The four
great truths of their religion[4] consist in the recognition of
the following principles : 1. that there is suffering ; 2. that
there is a cause of that suffering ; 3. that such cause can be
removed ; 4. that there is a way of deliverance, viz. the
doctrine of Buddha. This way is the ash*t*ânga-mârga,
the eightfold way[5], taught by Buddha, and leading to Nirvâ*n*a[6]. The faithful advances on that road, padât padam,

---

[1] See M. M.'s Sanskrit Grammar, § 519.

[2] Mr. D'Alwis' arguments (Buddhist Nirvâ*n*a, pp. 63–67) in support of this
view, viz. the dhammapada may be a collective term, do not seem to me to
strengthen my own conjecture.

[3] Dhammapada from Chinese, p. 4.

[4] Spence Hardy, Manual, p. 496.

[5] Burnouf, Lotus, p. 520, 'Ajoutons, pour terminer ce que nous trouvons à dire
sur le mot magga, quelque commentaire qu'on en donne d'ailleurs, que suivant
une définition rapportée par Turnour, le magga renferme une sous-division que
l'on nomme pa*t*ipadâ, en sanscrit prati̇pad. Le magga, dit Turnour, est la
voie qui conduit au Nibbâna, la pa*t*ipadâ, littéralement "la marche pas à pas,
ou le degré," est la vie de rectitude qu'on doit suivre, quand on marche dans la
voie du magga.'

[6] See Spence Hardy, Manual, p. 496. Should not *k*aturvidha-dharmapada,
mentioned on p. 497, be translated by 'the fourfold path of the Law?' It can
hardly be the fourfold word of the Law.

step by step, and it is therefore called pa*i*padâ, lit. the step by step.

If we make allowance for these ambiguities, inherent in the name of Dhammapada, we may well understand how the Buddhists themselves play with the word pada (see v. 45). Thus we read in Mr. Beal's translation of a Chinese version of the Prâtimoksha [1]:

> ' Let all those who desire such birth,
> Who now are living in the world,
> Guard and preserve these Precepts, as feet.'

TRANSLATION.

In translating the verses of the Dhammapada, I have followed the edition of the Pâli text, published in 1855 by Dr. Fausböll, and I have derived great advantage from his Latin translation, his notes, and his copious extracts from Buddhaghosa's commentary. I have also consulted translations, either of the whole of the Dhammapada, or of portions of it, by Burnouf, Gogerly [2], Upham, Weber, and others. Though it will be seen that in many places my translation differs from those of my predecessors, I can only claim for myself the name of a very humble gleaner in this field of Pâli literature. The greatest credit is due to Dr. Fausböll, whose editio princeps of the Dhammapada will mark for ever an important epoch in the history of Pâli scholarship ; and though later critics have been able to point out some mistakes, both in his text and in his translation, the value of their labours is not to be compared with that of the work accomplished single-handed by that eminent Danish scholar.

In revising my translation, first published in 1870 [3], for

---

[1] Catena, p. 207.

[2] 'Several of the chapters have been translated by Mr. Gogerly, and have appeared in The Friend, vol. iv, 1840.' (Spence Hardy, Eastern Monachism, p. 169.)

[3] Buddhaghosha's Parables, translated from Burmese by Captain T. Rogers, R. E. With an Introduction, containing Buddha's Dhammapada, translated from Pâli by F. Max Müller. London, 1870.

the Sacred Books of the East, I have been able to avail myself of 'Notes on Dhammapada,' published by Childers in the Journal of the Royal Asiatic Society (May, 1871), and of valuable hints as to the meaning of certain words and verses scattered about in the Pâli Dictionary of that much regretted scholar, 1875. I have carefully weighed the remarks of Mr. James D'Alwis in his 'Buddhist Nirvâna, a review of Max Müller's Dhammapada' (Colombo, 1871), and accepted some of his suggestions. Some very successful renderings of a number of verses by Mr. Rhys Davids in his 'Buddhism,' and a French translation, too, of the Dhammapada, published by Fernand Hû[1], have been consulted with advantage.

It was hoped for a time that much assistance for a more accurate understanding of this work might be derived from a Chinese translation of the Dhammapada[2], of which Mr. S. Beal published an English translation in 1878. But this hope has not been entirely fulfilled. It was, no doubt, a discovery of great interest, when Mr. Beal announced that the text of the Dhammapada was not restricted to the southern Buddhists only, but that similar collections existed in the north, and had been translated into Chinese. It was equally important when Schiefner proved the existence of the same work in the sacred canon of the Tibetans. But as yet neither a Chinese nor a Tibetan translation of the Pâli Dhammapada has been rendered accessible to us by translations of these translations into English or German, and what we have received instead, cannot make up for what we had hoped for.

The state of the case is this. There are, as Mr. Beal informs us, four principal copies of what may be called Dhammapada in Chinese, the first dating from the Wu dynasty, about the beginning of the third century A.D. This translation, called Fa-kheu-king, is the work of a

---

[1] Le Dhammapada avec introduction et notes par Fernand Hû, suivi du Sutra en 42 articles, traduit du Tibetain, par Léon Feer. Paris, 1878.

[2] Texts from the Buddhist Canon, commonly known as Dhammapada, translated from the Chinese by Samuel Beal. London, 1878.

Shaman Wei-*k*i-lan and others. Its title means 'the Sûtra of Law verses,' kheu being explained by gâthâ, a verse, a word which we shall meet with again in the Tibetan title, Gâthâsaṅgraha. In the preface the Chinese translator states that the Shamans in after ages copied from the canonical scriptures various gâthâs, some of four lines and some of six, and attached to each set of verses a title, according to the subject therein explained. This work of extracting and collecting is ascribed to Tsun-*k*e-Fa-kieou, i. e. Ârya-Dharmatrâta, the author of the Sa*m*yuktâbhidharma-*s*âstra and other works, and the uncle of Vasumitra. If this Vasumitra was the patriarch who took a prominent part in the Council under Kanishka, Dharmatrâta's collection would belong to the first century B.C.; but this is, as yet, very doubtful.

In the preface to the Fa-kheu-king we are told that the original, which consisted of 500 verses, was brought from India by Wai-*k*i-lan in 223 A.D., and that it was translated into Chinese with the help of another Indian called Tsiang-sin. After the translation was finished, thirteen sections were added, making up the whole to 752 verses, 14,580 words, and 39 chapters[1].

If the Chinese translation is compared with the Pâli text, it appears that the two agree from the 9th to the 35th chapter (with the exception of the 33rd), so far as their subjects are concerned, though the Chinese has in these chapters 79 verses more than the Pâli. But the Chinese translation has eight additional chapters in the beginning (viz. On Intemperance, Inciting to Wisdom, The *S*râvaka, Simple Faith, Observance of Duty, Reflection, Loving-kindness, Conversation), and four at the end (viz. Nirvâ*n*a, Birth and Death, Profit of Religion, and Good Fortune), and one between the 24th and 25th chapter of the Pâli text (viz. Advantageous Service), all of which are absent in our Pâli texts. This, the most ancient

---

[1] Beal, Dhammapada, p. 30. The real number of verses, however, is 760. In the Pâli text, too, there are five verses more than stated in the Index; see M. M., Buddhaghosha's Parables, p. ix, note; Beal, loc. cit. p. 11, note.

Chinese translation of Dharmatrâta's work, has not been
rendered into English by Mr. Beal, but he assures us that
it is a faithful reproduction of the original. The book which
he has chosen for translation is the Fa-kheu-pi-ü, i. e.
parables connected with the Dhammapada, and translated
into Chinese by two Shamans of the western Tsin dynasty
(A.D. 265–313). These parables are meant to illustrate the
teaching of the verses, like the parables of Buddhaghosa,
but they are not the same parables, nor do they illustrate
all the verses.

A third Chinese version is called *K*uh-yan-king, i. e. the
Sûtra of the Dawn (avadâna?), consisting of seven, volumes.
Its author was Dharmatrâta, its translator *K*u-fo-nien (Bud-
dhasmr*i*ti), about 410 A.D. The MS. of the work is said
to have been brought from India by a Shaman Saṅgha-
bhadaṅga of Kipin (Cabul), about 345 A.D. It is a much
more extensive work in 33 chapters, the last being, as in
the Pâli text, on the Brâhma*n*a.

A fourth translation dates from the Sung dynasty (800
or 900 A.D.), and in it, too, the authorship of the text is
ascribed to Ârya-Dharmatrâta.

A Tibetan translation of a Dhammapada was discovered by Schiefner in the 28th volume of the Sûtras,
in the collection called Udânavarga. It contains 33
chapters, and more than 1000 verses, of which about one-
fourth only can be traced in the Pâli text. The same
collection is found also in the Tang*u*r, vol. 71 of the Sûtras,
foll. 1–53, followed by a commentary, the Udânavarga-
vivara*n*a by the Â*k*ârya Prag*n*âvarman. Unfortunately
Schiefner's intention of publishing a translation of it (Mélanges Asiatiques, tom. viii. p. 560) has been frustrated by
his death. All that he gives us in his last paper is the
Tibetan text with translation of another shorter collection,
the Gâthâsaṅgraha by Vasubandhu, equally published in
the 72nd volume of the Sûtras in the Tang*u*r, and accom-
panied by a commentary.

SPELLING OF BUDDHIST TERMS.

I had on a former occasion[1] pleaded so strongly in favour of retaining, as much as possible, the original Sanskrit forms of Pâli Buddhist terms, that I feel bound to confess openly that I hold this opinion no longer, or, at all events, that I see it is hopeless to expect that Pâli scholars will accept my proposal. My arguments were these : 'Most of the technical terms employed by Buddhist writers come from Sanskrit ; and in the eyes of the philologist the various forms which they have assumed in Pâli, in Burmese, in Tibetan, in Chinese, in Mongolian, are only so many corruptions of the same original form. Everything, therefore, would seem to be in favour of retaining the Sanskrit forms throughout, and of writing, for instance, Nirvâ*n*a instead of the Pâli Nibbâna, the Burmese Niban or Nepbhân, the Siamese Niruphan, the Chinese Nipan. The only hope, in fact, that writers on Buddhism will ever arrive at a uniform and generally intelligible phraseology seems to lie in their agreeing to use throughout the Sanskrit terms in their original form, instead of the various local disguises and disfigurements which they present in Ceylon, Burmah, Siam, Tibet, China, and Mongolia.'

I fully admitted that many Buddhist words have assumed such a strongly marked local or national character in the different countries and in the different languages in which the religion of Buddha has found a new home, that to translate them back into Sanskrit might seem as affected, nay, prove in certain cases as misleading, as if, in speaking of priests and kings, we were to speak of presbyters and cynings. The rule by which I meant mainly to be guided was to use the Sanskrit forms as much as possible ; in fact, everywhere except where it seemed affected to do so. I therefore wrote Buddhaghosha instead of the Pâli Buddhaghosa, because the name of that famous theologian, 'the Voice of Buddha,' seemed to lose its significance if turned

---

[1] Introduction to Buddhaghosha's Parables, 1870, p. l.

into Buddhaghosa. But I was well aware what may be said on the other side. The name of Buddhaghosa, 'Voice of Buddha,' was given him after he had been converted from Brahmanism to Buddhism, and it was given to him by people to whom the Pâli word g h o s a conveyed the same meaning as g h o s h a does to us. On the other hand, I retained the Pâli D h a m m a p a d a instead of Dharmapada, simply because, as the title of a Pâli book, it has become so familiar that to speak of it as Dharmapada seemed like speaking of another work. We are accustomed to speak of Samanas instead of *S*rama*n*as, for even in the days of Alexander's conquest, the Sanskrit word *S*rama*n*a had assumed the prakritized or vulgar form which we find in Pâli, and which alone could have been rendered by the later Greek writers (first by Alexander Polyhistor, 80–60 B. C.) by σαμαναῖοι [1]. As a Buddhist term, the Pâli form Samana has so entirely supplanted that of *S*rama*n*a that, even in the Dhammapada (v. 388), we find an etymology of Samana as derived from sam, 'to be quiet,' and not from *s*ram, 'to toil.' But if we speak of Samanas, we ought also to speak of Bâhma*n*as instead of Brâhma*n*as, for this word had been replaced by bâhma*n*a at so early a time, that in the Dhammapada it is derived from a root vah, 'to remove, to separate, to cleanse [2].'

I still believe that it would be best if writers on Buddhist literature and religion were to adopt Sanskrit throughout as the lingua franca. For an accurate understanding of the original meaning of most of the technical terms of Buddhism a knowledge of their Sanskrit form is indispensable; and nothing is lost, while much would be gained, if, even in the treating of southern Buddhism, we were to

---

[1] See Lassen, Indische Alterthumskunde, vol. ii. p. 700, note. That Lassen is right in taking the Σαρμᾶναι, mentioned by Megasthenes, for Brahmanic, not for Buddhist ascetics, might be proved also by their dress. Dresses made of the bark of trees are not strictly Buddhistic.

[2] See Dhammapada, v. 388; Bastian, Völker des östlichen Asien, vol. iii. p. 412: 'Ein buddhistischer Mönch erklärte mir, dass die Brahmanen ihren Namen führten, als Leute, die ihre Sünden abgespült hätten.' See also Lalitavistara, p. 551, line 1; p. 553, line 7.

speak of the town of Srâvastî instead of Sâvatthi in Pâli, Sevet in Sinhalese ; of Tripiṭaka, 'the three baskets,' instead of Tipiṭaka in Pâli, Tunpitaka in Sinhalese; of Arthakathâ, 'commentary,' instead of Aṭṭhakathâ in Pâli, Atuwâva in Sinhalese ; and therefore also of Dharmapada, 'the path of virtue,' instead of Dhammapada.

But inclinations are stronger than arguments. Pâli scholars prefer their Pâli terms, and I cannot blame them for it. Mr. D'Alwis (Buddhist Nirvâṇa, p. 68) says : 'It will be seen how very difficult it is to follow the rule rigidly. We are, therefore, inclined to believe that in translating Pâli works, at least, much inconvenience may not be felt by the retention of the forms of the language in which the Buddhist doctrines were originally delivered.' For the sake of uniformity, therefore, I have given up my former plan. I use the Pâli forms when I quote from Pâli, but I still prefer the Sanskrit forms, not only when I quote from Sanskrit Buddhist books, but also when I have to speak of Buddhism in general. I speak of Nirvâṇa, dharma, and bhikshu, rather than of Nibbâna, dhamma, and bhikkhu, when discussing the meaning of these words without special reference to southern Buddhism ; but when treating of the literature and religion of the Theravâda school I must so far yield to the arguments of Pâli scholars as to admit that it is but fair to use their language when speaking of their opinions.

DHAMMAPADA.

DHAMMAPADA.

CHAPTER I.

THE TWIN-VERSES.

1. All that we are is the result of what we have thought: it is founded on our thoughts, it is made up of our thoughts. If a man speaks or acts with an evil thought, pain follows him, as the wheel follows the foot of the ox that draws the carriage.

---

1. Dharma, though clear in its meaning, is difficult to translate. It has different meanings in different systems of philosophy, and its peculiar application in the phraseology of Buddhism has been fully elucidated by Burnouf, Introduction à l'Histoire du Buddhisme, p. 41 seq. He writes: 'Je traduis ordinairement ce terme par condition, d'autres fois par lois, mais aucune de ces traductions n'est parfaitement complète; il faut entendre par dharma ce qui fait qu'une chose est ce qu'elle est, ce qui constitue sa nature propre, comme l'a bien montré Lassen, à l'occasion de la célèbre formule, "Ye dharmâ hetuprabhavâ."' Etymologically the Latin for-ma expresses the same general idea which was expressed by dhar-ma. See also Burnouf, Lotus de la bonne Loi, p. 524. Fausböll translates: 'Naturae a mente principium ducunt,' which shows that he rightly understood dharma in the Buddhist sense. Gogerly (see Spence Hardy, Eastern Monachism, p. 28) translates: 'Mind precedes action,' which, if not wrong, is at all events wrongly expressed; while Professor Weber's rendering, 'Die Pflichten aus dem Herz folgern,' is quite inadmissible. D'Alwis (Buddhist Nirwana, p. 70 seq.), following the commentary, proposes to give a more technical interpretation of this verse, viz. 'Mind is the leader of all its faculties. Mind is the chief (of all its faculties). The very mind is made up of those (faculties). If one speaks or acts with a polluted mind, then affliction follows him as the wheel follows the feet of the bearer (the bullock).' To me this technical acceptation

2. All that we are is the result of what we have thought: it is founded on our thoughts, it is made up of our thoughts. If a man speaks or acts with a pure thought, happiness follows him, like a shadow that never leaves him.

3. ' He abused me, he beat me, he defeated me, he robbed me,'—in those who harbour such thoughts hatred will never cease.

4. ' He abused me, he beat me, he defeated me, he robbed me,'—in those who do not harbour such thoughts hatred will cease.

---

seems not applicable here, where we have to deal with the simplest moral precepts, and not with psychological niceties of Buddhist philosophy. It should be stated, however, that Childers, who first (s. v. dhamma) approved of my translation, seems afterwards to have changed his opinion. On p. 120 of his excellent Pâli Dictionary he said: ' Three of the five khandhas, viz. vedanâ, saññâ, and saṅkhâra, are collectively termed dhammâ (plur.), "mental faculties," and in the first verse of Dhammapada the commentator takes the word dhammâ to mean those three faculties. But this interpretation appears forced and unnatural, and I look upon Dr. Max Müller's translation, " All that we are is the result of what we have thought," as the best possible rendering of the spirit of the phrase mano pubbaṅgamâ dhammâ.' But on p. 577 the same scholar writes: ' Of the four mental khandhas the superiority of viññâṇa is strongly asserted in the first verse of Dhammapada, " The mental faculties (vedanâ, saññâ, and saṅkhâra) are dominated by Mind, they are governed by Mind, they are made up of Mind." That this is the true meaning of the passage I am now convinced ; see D'Alwis, Nirwana, pp. 70–75.' I do not deny that this may have been the traditional interpretation, at all events since the days of Buddhaghosa, but the very legend quoted by Buddhaghosa in illustration of this verse shows that its simpler and purely moral interpretation was likewise supported by tradition, and I therefore adhere to my original translation.

2. See Beal, Dhammapada, p. 169.

3. On akkokkhi, see Kakkâyana VI, 4, 17. D'Alwis, Pâli Grammar, p. 38 note. ' When akkokkhi means "he abused," it is derived from krus, not from krudh.' See Senart, Kakkâyana, l. c.

5. For hatred does not cease by hatred at any time: hatred ceases by love, this is an old rule.

6. The world does not know that we must all come to an end here ;—but those who know it, their quarrels cease at once.

7. He who lives looking for pleasures only, his senses uncontrolled, immoderate in his food, idle, and weak, Mâra (the tempter) will certainly overthrow him, as the wind throws down a weak tree.

8. He who lives without looking for pleasures, his senses well controlled, moderate in his food, faithful and strong, him Mâra will certainly not overthrow, any more than the wind throws down a rocky mountain.

9. He who wishes to put on the yellow dress without having cleansed himself from sin, who disregards also temperance and truth, is unworthy of the yellow dress.

---

6. Pare is explained by 'fools,' but it has that meaning by implication only. It is οἱ πόλλοι, cf. Vinaya, ed. Oldenberg, vol. i. p. 5, l. 4. Yamâmase, a 1 pers. plur. imp. Âtm., but really a Le/ in Pâli. See Fausböll, Five Gâtakas, p. 38.

7. Mâra must be taken in the Buddhist sense of 'tempter,' or 'evil spirit.' See Burnouf, Introduction, p. 76 : 'Mâra est le démon de l'amour, du péché et de la mort ; c'est le tentateur et l'ennemi de Buddha.' As to the definite meaning of vîrya, see Burnouf, Lotus, p. 548.

In the Buddhistical Sanskrit, kusîda, 'idle,' is the exact counterpart of the Pâli kusîta ; see Burnouf, Lotus, p. 548. On the change of Sanskrit d into Pâli t, see Kuhn, Beiträge zur Pali Grammatik, p. 40; Weber, Ind. Studien, XIII, p. 135.

9. The dark yellow dress, the Kâsâva or Kâshâya, is the distinctive garment of the Buddhist priests. See Vishnu-sûtra LXIII, 36. The play on the words anikkasâvo kâsâvam, or in Sanskrit anishkashâya/ kâshâyam, cannot be rendered in English. Kashâya means ' impurity,' nish-kashâya, ' free from impurity,' anish-kashâya, ' not free from impurity,' while kâshâya is the name of the yellowish

10. But he who has cleansed himself from sin, is well grounded in all virtues, and regards also temperance and truth, he is indeed worthy of the yellow dress.

11. They who imagine truth in untruth, and see untruth in truth, never arrive at truth, but follow vain desires.

12. They who know truth in truth, and untruth in untruth, arrive at truth, and follow true desires.

13. As rain breaks through an ill-thatched house, passion will break through an unreflecting mind.

14. As rain does not break through a well-thatched house, passion will not break through a well-reflecting mind.

15. The evil-doer mourns in this world, and he

Buddhist garment. The pun is evidently a favourite one, for, as Fausböll shows, it occurs also in the Mahâbhârata, XII, 568 :

Anishkashâye kâshâyam îhârtham iti viddhi tam,
Dharmadhvagânâm mundânâm vrittyartham iti me matih.

'Know that this yellow-coloured garment on a man who is not free from impurity, serves only for the purpose of cupidity ; my opinion is, that it is meant to supply the means of living to those shavelings, who carry their virtue or the dharma like a flag.'

(I read vrittyartham, according to the Bombay edition, instead of krîârtham, the reading of the Calcutta edition.)

On the exact colour of the dress, see Bishop Bigandet, The Life or Legend of Gaudama, the Budha of the Burmese, Rangoon, 1866, p. 504. Cf. Gâtaka, vol. ii. p. 198.

10. With regard to sîla, 'virtue,' see Burnouf, Lotus, p. 547.

11, 12. Sâra, which I have translated by 'truth,' has many meanings in Sanskrit. It means the sap of a thing, then essence or reality ; in a metaphysical sense, the highest reality ; in a moral sense, truth. It is impossible in a translation to do more than indicate the meaning of such words, and in order to understand them fully, we must know not only their definition, but their history. See Beal, Dhammapada, p. 64.

13. See Beal, Dhammapada, p. 65.

15. Kilittha is klishta, a participle of klis. It means literally,

mourns in the next; he mourns in both. He mourns and suffers when he sees the evil of his own work.

16. The virtuous man delights in this world, and he delights in the next; he delights in both. He delights and rejoices, when he sees the purity of his own work.

17. The evil-doer suffers in this world, and he suffers in the next; he suffers in both. He suffers when he thinks of the evil he has done; he suffers more when going on the evil path.

18. The virtuous man is happy in this world, and he is happy in the next; he is happy in both. He is happy when he thinks of the good he has done; he is still more happy when going on the good path.

19. The thoughtless man, even if he can recite a large portion (of the law), but is not a doer of it, has no share in the priesthood, but is like a cowherd counting the cows of others.

---

what is spoilt. The abstract noun kleṣa, 'evil or sin,' is constantly employed in Buddhist works; see Burnouf, Lotus, p. 443.

16. Like klishṭa in the preceding verse, viṣuddhi in the present has a technical meaning. One of Buddhaghosa's most famous works is called Visuddhi-magga. See Burnouf, Lotus, p. 844; Beal, Dhammapada, p. 67.

17, 18. 'The evil path and the good path' are technical expressions for the descending and ascending scale of worlds through which all beings have to travel upward or downward, according to their deeds; see Bigandet, Life of Gaudama, p. 5, note 4, and p. 449; Burnouf, Introduction, p. 599; Lotus, p. 865, l. 7; l. 11. Fausböll translates 'heaven and hell,' which comes to the same; cf. vv. 126, 306.

19. In taking sahitam in the sense of saṃhitam or saṃhitâ, I follow the commentator who says, Tepiṭakassa Buddhavaḳanass' etaṃ nâmaṃ, but I cannot find another passage where the Tipiṭaka, or any portion of it, is called Sahita. Saṃhita in vv. 100-102 has a different meaning. The fact that some followers of Buddha were

20. The follower of the law, even if he can recite only a small portion (of the law), but, having forsaken passion and hatred and foolishness, possesses true knowledge and serenity of mind, he, caring for nothing in this world or that to come, has indeed a share in the priesthood.

---

allowed to learn short portions only of the sacred writings by heart, and to repeat them, while others had to learn a larger collection, is shown by the story of *K*akkhupâla, p. 3, of Mahâkâla, p. 26, &c. See Childers, s. v. sahita.

20. Sâma*ññ*a, which I have rendered by 'priesthood,' expresses all that belongs to, or constitutes a real Sama*n*a or *S*rama*n*a, this being the Buddhist name corresponding to the Brâhma*n*a, or priest, of the orthodox Hindus. Buddha himself is frequently called the Good Sama*n*a. Fausböll takes the abstract word sâma*ññ*a as corresponding to the Sanskrit sâmânya, 'community,' but Weber has well shown that it ought to be taken as representing *s*râma*n*ya. He might have quoted the Sâma*ññ*a-phala-sutta, of which Burnouf has given such interesting details in his Lotus, p. 449 seq. Fausböll also, in his notes on v. 332, rightly explains sâma*ññ*atâ by *s*râma*n*yatâ. See Childers, s. v. sâma*ññ*a.

Anupâdiyâno, which I have translated by 'caring for nothing,' has a technical meaning. It is the negative of the fourth Nidâna, the so-called Upâdâna, which Köppen has well explained by Anhänglichkeit, 'taking to the world, loving the world.' Köppen, Die Religion des Buddha, p. 610. Cf. Suttanipâta, v. 470.

CHAPTER II.

ON EARNESTNESS [1].

21. Earnestness is the path of immortality (Nirvâna), thoughtlessness the path of death. Those who are in earnest do not die, those who are thoughtless are as if dead already.

22. Those who are advanced in earnestness, having understood this clearly, delight in earnestness, and rejoice in the knowledge of the Ariyas (the elect).

23. These wise people, meditative, steady, always possessed of strong powers, attain to Nirvâna, the highest happiness.

---

[1] There is nothing in the tenth section of the Dhammapada, as translated by Beal, corresponding to the verses of this chapter.

21. Apramâda, which Fausböll translates by 'vigilantia,' Gogerly by 'religion,' Childers by 'diligence,' expresses literally the absence of that giddiness or thoughtlessness which characterizes the state of mind of worldly people. It is the first entering into oneself, and hence all virtues are said to have their root in apramâda. (Ye keki kusalâ dhammâ sabbe te appamâdamûlakâ.) I have translated it by 'earnestness,' sometimes by 'reflection.' 'Immortality,' amrita, is explained by Buddhaghosa as Nirvâna. Amrita is used, no doubt, as a synonym of Nirvâna, but this very fact shows how many different conceptions entered from the very first into the Nirvâna of the Buddhists. See Childers, s. v. nibbâna, p. 269.

This verse, as recited to Asoka, occurs in the Dîpavamsa VI, 53, and in the Mahâvamsa, p. 25. See also Sanatsugâtîya, translated by Telang, Sacred Books of the East, vol. viii. p. 138.

22. The Ariyas, the noble or elect, are those who have entered on the path that leads to Nirvâna; see Köppen, p. 396. Their knowledge and general status is minutely described; see Köppen, p. 436.

23. Childers, s. v. nibbâna, thinks that nibbâna here and in many other places means Arhatship.

[10]   e

24. If an earnest person has roused himself, if he is not forgetful, if his deeds are pure, if he acts with consideration, if he restrains himself, and lives according to law,—then his glory will increase.

25. By rousing himself, by earnestness, by restraint and control, the wise man may make for himself an island which no flood can overwhelm.

26. Fools follow after vanity, men of evil wisdom. The wise man keeps earnestness as his best jewel.

27. Follow not after vanity, nor after the enjoyment of love and lust! He who is earnest and meditative, obtains ample joy.

28. When the learned man drives away vanity by earnestness, he, the wise, climbing the terraced heights of wisdom, looks down upon the fools, serene he looks upon the toiling crowd, as one that stands on a mountain looks down upon them that stand upon the plain.

29. Earnest among the thoughtless, awake among the sleepers, the wise man advances like a racer, leaving behind the hack.

30. By earnestness did Maghavan (Indra) rise to the lordship of the gods. People praise earnestness; thoughtlessness is always blamed.

31. A Bhikshu (mendicant) who delights in earnestness, who looks with fear on thoughtless-

---

25. Childers explains this island again as the state of an Arhat (arahatta-phalam).

28. Cf. Childers, Dictionary, Preface, p. xiv. See Vinaya, ed. Oldenberg, vol. i. p. 5, s. f.

31. Instead of saha*m*, which Dr. Fausböll translates by 'vincens,' Dr. Weber by 'conquering,' I think we ought to read *d*ahan, 'burning,' which was evidently the reading adopted by Buddha-

ness, moves about like fire, burning all his fetters, small or large.

32. A Bhikshu (mendicant) who delights in reflection, who looks with fear on thoughtlessness, cannot fall away (from his perfect state)—he is close upon Nirvâ*n*a.

---

ghosa. Mr. R. C. Childers, whom I requested to see whether the MS. at the India Office gives saha*m* or *d*aha*m*, writes that the reading *d*aha*m* is as clear as possible in that MS. The fetters are meant for the senses. See verse 370.

32. See Childers, Notes, p. 5.

CHAPTER III.

THOUGHT.

33. As a fletcher makes straight his arrow, a wise man makes straight his trembling and unsteady thought, which is difficult to guard, difficult to hold back,

34. As a fish taken from his watery home and thrown on the dry ground, our thought trembles all over in order to escape the dominion of Mâra (the tempter).

35. It is good to tame the mind, which is difficult to hold in and flighty, rushing wherever it listeth; a tamed mind brings happiness.

36. Let the wise man guard his thoughts, for they are difficult to perceive, very artful, and they rush wherever they list: thoughts well guarded bring happiness.

37. Those who bridle their mind which travels far, moves about alone, is without a body, and hides in the chamber (of the heart), will be free from the bonds of Mâra (the tempter).

38. If a man's thoughts are unsteady, if he does not know the true law, if his peace of mind is troubled, his knowledge will never be perfect.

39. If a man's thoughts are not dissipated, if

33. Cf. *Gâtaka*, vol. i. p. 400.
34. On Mâra, see verses 7 and 8.
35-39. Cf. *Gâtaka*, vol. i. pp. 312, 400.
39. Fausböll traces anavassuta, 'dissipated,' back to the Sanskrit

his mind is not perplexed, if he has ceased to think of good or evil, then there is no fear for him while he is watchful.

root *s*yai, 'to become rigid;' but the participle of that root would be *s*îta, not *s*yuta. Professor Weber suggests that anavassuta stands for the Sanskrit anavasruta, which he translates unbefleckt, 'unspotted.' If avasruta were the right word, it might be taken in the sense of 'not fallen off, not fallen away,' but it could not mean 'unspotted;' cf. dhairya*m* no 'susruvat, 'our firmness ran away.' I have little doubt, however, that avassuta represents the Sanskrit ava*s*ruta, and is derived from the root *s*ru, here used in its technical sense, peculiar to the Buddhist literature, and so well explained by Burnouf in his Appendix XIV (Lotus, p. 820). He shows that, according to Hema*k*andra and the *G*ina-alankâra, â*s*ravakshaya, Pâli âsavasa*m*khaya is counted as the sixth abhi*g*ñâ, wherever six of these intellectual powers are mentioned, instead of five. The Chinese translate the term in their own Chinese fashion by 'stillationis finis,' but Burnouf claims for it the definite sense of destruction of faults or vices. He quotes from the Lalita-vistara (Adhyâya XXII, ed. Râjendra Lal Mittra, p. 448) the words uttered by Buddha when he arrived at his complete Buddhahood :—

*S*ushkâ â*s*ravâ na puna*h s*ravanti,

'The vices are dried up, they will not flow again;' and he shows that the Pâli Dictionary, the Abhidhânappadîpikâ, explains âsava simply by kâma, 'love, pleasure of the senses.' In the Mahâparinibbâna-sutta, three classes of âsava are distinguished, the kâmâsavâ, the bhavâsavâ, and the avi*gg*âsavâ. See also Burnouf, Lotus, p. 665; Childers, s. v. âsavo.

That *s*ru means 'to run,' and is in fact a merely dialectic variety of sru, has been proved by Burnouf, while Boehtlingk thinks the substitution of *s* for s is a mistake. Âsrava therefore, or âsrava, meant originally 'the running out towards objects of the senses' (cf. sanga, âlaya, &c.), and had nothing to do with âsrâva, 'a running, a sore,' Atharva-veda I, 2, 4. This conception of the original purport of â + *s*ru or ava-*s*ru is confirmed by a statement of Colebrooke's, who, when treating of the *G*ainas, writes (Miscellaneous Essays, I, 382): 'Âsrava is that which directs the embodied spirit (âsravayati purusham) towards external objects. It is the occupation and employment (vr*i*tti or pravr*i*tti) of the senses or organs on sensible objects. Through the means of the senses it

40. Knowing that this body is (fragile) like a
jar, and making this thought firm like a fortress,
one should attack Mâra (the tempter) with the
weapon of knowledge, one should watch him when
conquered, and should never rest.

41. Before long, alas! this body will lie on the
earth, despised, without understanding, like a use-
less log.

42. Whatever a hater may do to a hater, or

---

affects the embodied spirit with the sentiment of taction, colour,
smell, and taste. Or it is the association or connection of body
with right and wrong deeds. It comprises all the karmas, for they
(âsravayanti) pervade, influence, and attend the doer, following him
or attaching to him. It is a misdirection (mithyâ-pravṛtti) of the
organs, for it is vain, a cause of disappointment, rendering the
organs of sense and sensible objects subservient to fruition. Sam-
vara is that which stops (samvṛinoti) the course of the foregoing,
or closes up the door or passage to it, and consists in self-com-
mand or restraint of organs internal and external, embracing all
means of self-control and subjection of the senses, calming and
subduing them.'

For a full account of the âsravas, see Lalita-vistara, ed. Calc.
pp. 445 and 552, where Kshînâsrava is given as a name of Buddha.
Âsrâva occurs in Âpastamba's Dharma-sûtras II, 5, 9, where the
commentator explains it by objects of the senses, by which the
soul is made to run out. It is better, however, to take âsrâva
here, too, as the act of running out, the affections, appetites,
passions.

40. Anivesana has no doubt a technical meaning, and may
signify, one who has left his house, his family and friends, to
become a monk. A monk shall not return to his home, but travel
about; he shall be anivesana, 'homeless,' anâgâra, 'houseless.'
But I doubt whether this can be the meaning of anivesana here,
as the sentence, let him be an anchorite, would come in too
abruptly. I translate it therefore in a more general sense, let him
not return or turn away from the battle, let him watch Mâra, even
after he is vanquished, let him keep up a constant fight against the
adversary, without being attached to anything or anybody.

an enemy to an enemy, a wrongly-directed mind will do us greater mischief.

43. Not a mother, not a father will do so much, nor any other relative; a well-directed mind will do us greater service.

43. See Beal, Dhammapada, p. 73.

CHAPTER IV.

FLOWERS[1].

44. Who shall overcome this earth, and the world of Yama (the lord of the departed), and the world of the gods? Who shall find out the plainly shown path of virtue, as a clever man finds out the (right) flower?

45. The disciple will overcome the earth, and the world of Yama, and the world of the gods. The disciple will find out the plainly shown path of virtue, as a clever man finds out the (right) flower.

---

[1] See Beal, Dhammapada, p. 75.

44, 45. If I differ from the translation of Fausböll and Weber, it is because the commentary takes the two verbs, vigessati and pakessati, to mean in the end the same thing, i.e. sakkhi-karissati, 'he will perceive.' I have not ventured to take vigessate for viganissati, though it should be remembered that the overcoming of the earth and of the worlds below and above, as here alluded to, is meant to be achieved by means of knowledge. Pakessati, 'he will gather' (cf. vi-ki, Indische Sprüche, 4560), means also, like 'to gather' in English, 'he will perceive or understand,' and the dhammapada, or 'path of virtue,' is distinctly explained by Buddhaghosa as consisting of the thirty-seven states or stations which lead to Bodhi. (See Burnouf, Lotus, p. 430; Hardy, Manual, p. 497.) Dhammapada might, no doubt, mean also 'a law-verse,' and sudesita, 'well taught,' and this double meaning may be intentional here as elsewhere. Buddha himself is called Mârga-darsaka and Mârga-desika (cf. Lal. Vist. p. 551). There is a curious similarity between these verses and verses 6540-41, and 9939 of the Sânti-parva:

Pushpâniva vikinvantam anyatragatamanasam,
Anavâpteshu kâmeshu mrityur abhyeti mânavam.

'Death approaches man like one who is gathering flowers, and

46. He who knows that this body is like froth, and has learnt that it is as unsubstantial as a mirage, will break the flower-pointed arrow of Mâra, and never see the king of death.

47. Death carries off a man who is gathering flowers and whose mind is distracted, as a flood carries off a sleeping village.

48. Death subdues a man who is gathering flowers, and whose mind is distracted, before he is satiated in his pleasures.

49. As the bee collects nectar and departs without injuring the flower, or its colour or scent, so let a sage dwell in his village.

50. Not the perversities of others, not their sins

---

whose mind is turned elsewhere, before his desires have been fulfilled.'

Suptam vyâghram mahaugho vâ mrityur âdâya gakkhati, Sankinvânakam evainam kâmânâm avitriptikam.

' As a stream (carries off) a sleeping tiger, death carries off this man who is gathering flowers, and who is not satiated in his pleasures.'

This last verse, particularly, seems to me clearly a translation from Pâli, and the kam of sankinvânakam looks as if put in metri causâ.

46. The flower-arrows of Mâra, the tempter, are borrowed from Kâma, the Hindu god of love. For a similar expression see Lalita-vistara, ed. Calc. p. 40, l. 20, mâyâmarikisadrisâ vidyutphe-nopamâs kapalâh. It is on account of this parallel passage that I prefer to translate mariki by 'mirage,' and not by 'sunbeam,' as Fausböll, or by 'solar atom,' as Weber proposes. The expression, ' he will never see the king of death,' is supposed to mean Arhatship by Childers, s. v. nibbâna, p. 270.

47. See Thiessen, Die Legende von Kisâgotamî, p. 9.

48. Antaka, 'death,' is given as an explanation of Mâra in the Amarakosha and Abhidhânappadîpika (cf. Fausböll, p. 210).

49. See Beal, Catena, p. 159, where vv. 49 and 50 are ascribed to Wessabhu, i. e. Visvabhû. See also Der Weise und der Thor, p. 134.

of commission or omission, but his own misdeeds and negligences should a sage take notice of.

51. Like a beautiful flower, full of colour, but without scent, are the fine but fruitless words of him who does not act accordingly.

52. But, like a beautiful flower, full of colour and full of scent, are the fine and fruitful words of him who acts accordingly.

53. As many kinds of wreaths can be made from a heap of flowers, so many good things may be achieved by a mortal when once he is born.

54. The scent of flowers does not travel against the wind, nor (that of) sandal-wood, or of Tagara and Mallikâ flowers; but the odour of good people travels even against the wind; a good man pervades every place.

55. Sandal-wood or Tagara, a lotus-flower, or a Vassikî, among these sorts of perfumes, the perfume of virtue is unsurpassed.

56. Mean is the scent that comes from Tagara and sandal-wood;—the perfume of those who possess virtue rises up to the gods as the highest.

57. Of the people who possess these virtues, who live without thoughtlessness, and who are emanci-

---

51. St. Matthew xxiii. 3, 'For they say, and do not.'

54. Tagara, a plant from which a scented powder is made. Mallaka or mallikâ, according to Benfey, is an oil vessel. Hence tagaramallikâ was supposed to mean a bottle holding aromatic powder, or oil made of the Tagara. Mallikâ, however, is given by Dr. Eitel (Handbook of Chinese Buddhism) as the name of a flower now called Casturi (musk) on account of its rich odour, and Dr. Morris informs me that he has found mallikâ in Pâli as a name of jasmine. See also Childers, s. v.; Notes, p. 6; and Beal, Dhammapada, p. 76.

pated through true knowledge, Mâra, the tempter, never finds the way.

58, 59. As on a heap of rubbish cast upon the highway the lily will grow full of sweet perfume and delight, thus the disciple of the truly enlightened Buddha shines forth by his knowledge among those who are like rubbish, among the people that walk in darkness.

58, 59. Cf. Beal, Dhammapada, p. 76.

CHAPTER V.

THE FOOL.

60. Long is the night to him who is awake ; long is a mile to him who is tired ; long is life to the foolish who do not know the true law.

61. If a traveller does not meet with one who is his better, or his equal, let him firmly keep to his solitary journey ; there is no companionship with a fool.

62. ' These sons belong to me, and this wealth belongs to me,' with such thoughts a fool is tormented. He himself does not belong to himself ; how much less sons and wealth ?

63. The fool who knows his foolishness, is wise at least so far. But a fool who thinks himself wise, he is called a fool indeed.

64. If a fool be associated with a wise man even all his life, he will perceive the truth as little as a spoon perceives the taste of soup.

65. If an intelligent man be associated for one minute only with a wise man, he will soon perceive the truth, as the tongue perceives the taste of soup.

66. Fools of little understanding have themselves

---

60. ' Life,' sa*m*sâra, is the constant revolution of birth and death which goes on for ever until the knowledge of the true law or the true doctrine of Buddha enables a man to free himself from sa*m*sâra, and to enter into Nirvâ*na.* See Buddhaghosha's Parables, Parable XIX, p. 134.

61. Cf. Suttanipâta, v. 46.

63. Cf. Beal, Dhammapada, p. 77.

65. Cf. Beal, Dhammapada, p. 78.

for their greatest enemies, for they do evil deeds which must bear bitter fruits.

67. That deed is not well done of which a man must repent, and the reward of which he receives crying and with a tearful face.

68. No, that deed is well done of which a man does not repent, and the reward of which he receives gladly and cheerfully.

69. As long as the evil deed done does not bear fruit, the fool thinks it is like honey; but when it ripens, then the fool suffers grief.

70. Let a fool month after month eat his food (like an ascetic) with the tip of a blade of Kusa grass, yet is he not worth the sixteenth particle of those who have well weighed the law.

71. An evil deed, like newly-drawn milk, does not turn (suddenly); smouldering, like fire covered by ashes, it follows the fool.

67. See Beal, l.c. p. 78.

69. Taken from the Samyutta-nikâya, where, however, we read thânanhi instead of madhuvâ; see Feer, Comptes Rendus, 1871, p. 64.

70. The commentator clearly takes sankhâta in the sense of sankhyâta, 'reckoned,' for he explains it by ñâtadhammâ, tulita-dhammâ. The eating with the tip of Kusa grass has reference to the fastings performed by the Brahmans, but disapproved of, except as a moderate discipline, by the followers of Buddha. This verse seems to interrupt the continuity of the other verses which treat of the reward of evil deeds, or of the slow but sure ripening of every sinful act. See Childers, s. v. sankhâto.

71. I am not at all certain of the simile, unless mukkati, as applied to milk, can be used in the sense of changing or turning sour. In Manu IV, 172, where a similar sentence occurs, the commentators are equally doubtful: Nâdharmas karito loke sadyah phalati gaur iva, 'for an evil act committed in the world does not bear fruit at once, like a cow;' or 'like the earth (in due season);' or 'like milk.' See Childers, Notes, p. 6.

72. And when the evil deed, after it has become known, brings sorrow to the fool, then it destroys his bright lot, nay, it cleaves his head.

73. Let the fool wish for a false reputation, for precedence among the Bhikshus, for lordship in the convents, for worship among other people!

74. 'May both the layman and he who has left the world think that this is done by me; may they be subject to me in everything which is to be done or is not to be done,' thus is the mind of the fool, and his desire and pride increase.

75. 'One is the road that leads to wealth, another the road that leads to Nirvâna;' if the Bhikshu, the disciple of Buddha, has learnt this, he will not yearn for honour, he will strive after separation from the world.

---

72. I take *ñattam* for *gñapitam*, the causative of *gñâtam*, for which in Sanskrit, too, we have the form without i, *gñaptam*. This *gñaptam*, 'made known, revealed,' stands in opposition to the *khanna*, 'covered, hid,' of the preceding verse. Sukkamsa, which Fausböll explains by *suklâmsa*, has probably a more technical and special meaning. Childers traces *ñattam* to the Vedic *gñâtram*, 'knowledge.' Fausböll refers to *Gâtaka*, vol. i. p. 445, v. 118.

75. Viveka, which in Sanskrit means chiefly understanding, has with the Buddhists the more technical meaning of separation, whether separation from the world and retirement to the solitude of the forest (kâya-viveka), or separation from idle thoughts (*k*itta-viveka), or the highest separation and freedom (Nirvâna).

CHAPTER VI.

THE WISE MAN (PANDITA).

76. If you see an intelligent man who tells you where true treasures are to be found, who shows what is to be avoided, and administers reproofs, follow that wise man; it will be better, not worse, for those who follow him.

77. Let him admonish, let him teach, let him forbid what is improper !—he will be beloved of the good, by the bad he will be hated.

78. Do not have evil-doers for friends, do not have low people for friends : have virtuous people for friends, have for friends the best of men.

79. He who drinks in the law lives happily with a serene mind : the sage rejoices always in the law, as preached by the elect (Ariyas).

80. Well-makers lead the water (wherever they like); fletchers bend the arrow ; carpenters bend a log of wood ; wise people fashion themselves.

---

78. It is hardly possible to take mitte kalyâne in the technical sense of kalyâna-mitra, 'ein geistlicher Rath,' a spiritual guide. Burnouf (Introd. p. 284) shows that in the technical sense kalyâna-mitra was widely spread in the Buddhist world.

79. Ariya, 'elect, venerable,' is explained by the comméntator as referring to Buddha and other teachers.

80. See verses 33 and 145, the latter being a mere repetition of our verse. The nettikâs, to judge from the commentary and from the general purport of the verse, are not simply water-carriers, but builders of canals and aqueducts, who force the water to go where it would not go by itself. The Chinese translator says, 'the pilot manages his ship.' See Beal, l. c. p. 79.

81. As a solid rock is not shaken by the wind, wise people falter not amidst blame and praise.

82. Wise people, after they have listened to the laws, become serene, like a deep, smooth, and still lake.

83. Good people walk on whatever befall, the good do not prattle, longing for pleasure ; whether touched by happiness or sorrow wise people never appear elated or depressed.

84. If, whether for his own sake, or for the sake of others, a man wishes neither for a son, nor for wealth, nor for lordship, and if he does not wish for his own success by unfair means, then he is good, wise, and virtuous.

85. Few are there among men who arrive at the other shore (become Arhats); the other people here run up and down the shore.

---

83. The first line is very doubtful. I have adopted, in my translation, a suggestion of Mr. Childers, who writes, ‘I think it will be necessary to take sabbattha in the sense of “everywhere,” or “under every condition;”’ pañkakhandâdibhedesu, sabbadhammesu, says Buddhaghosha. I do not think we need assume that B. means the word vigahanti to be a synonym of vaganti. I would rather take the whole sentence together as a gloss upon the word vaganti : —vagantîti arahattañânena apakaddhantâ khandarâgam vigahanti ; vaganti means that, ridding themselves of lust by the wisdom which Arhatship confers, they cast it away.’ I am inclined to think the line means ‘the righteous walk on (unmoved) in all the conditions of life.’ Nindâ, pasamsâ, sukha, dukkha are four of the eight lokadhammas, or earthly conditions ; the remaining lokadhammas are lâbha, alâbha, yasa, ayasa.

In v. 245, passatâ, ‘by a man who sees,’ means ‘by a man who sees clearly or truly.’ In the same manner vrag may mean, not simply ‘to walk,’ but ‘to walk properly,’ or may be used synonymously with pravrag.

85. ‘The other shore’ is meant for Nirvâna, ‘this shore’ for common life. On reaching Nirvâna, the dominion of death is

86. But those who, when the law has been well
preache[d] ... n, follow the law, will pass across
[the] ... death, however difficult to over-

... nan should leave the dark state
... d follow the bright state (of the
... ing from his home to a home-
... in his retirement look for
... re seemed to be no enjoy-
... easures behind, and calling
... e man should purge himself
... he mind.
... l is well grounded in the
... ledge, who without cling-

... lies târitvâ, 'having crossed,' in
... k/udheyyam. Possibly pâram
... word, in the sense of over-

... or bad and good; cf. Sutta-
... ng one's home is the same
... me or family, an anâgâra,
... ate of viveka, or retirement (see
... ere before there seemed to be no pleasure
... sure is to be found, or vice versâ. A similar idea is
e ... essed in verse 99. See Burnouf, Lotus, p. 474, where he speaks
of 'Le plaisir de la satisfaction, né de la distinction.'
The five troubles or evils of the mind are passion, anger, ignorance, arrogance, pride; see Burnouf, Lotus, pp. 360, 443. As to
pariyodapeyya, see verse 183, and Lotus, pp. 523, 528; as to
akiñ/kano, see Mahâbh. XII, 6568, 1240.
89. The elements of knowledge are the seven Sambodhyañgas,
on which see Burnouf, Lotus, p. 796. D'Alwis explains them as
the thirty-seven Bodhipakkhiya-dhammâ. Khînâsavâ, which I have
translated by 'they whose frailties have been conquered,' may also
be taken in a more metaphysical sense, as explained in the note to
v. 39. The same applies to the other terms occurring in this verse,
such as âdâna, anupâdâya, &c. Dr. Fausböll seems inclined to

[10] f

ing to anything, rejoice in freedom from attachment,
whose appetites have been conquered, and who are
full of light, are free (even) in this world.

---

take âsava in this passage, and in the other passages where it
occurs, as the Pâli representative of âsraya. But âsraya, in Buddhist
phraseology, means rather the five organs of sense with manas,
'the soul,' and these are kept distinct from the âsavas, 'the inclinations, the appetites, passions, or vices.' The commentary on the
Abhidharma, when speaking of the Yogâkâras, says, ' En réunissant
ensemble les réceptacles (âsraya), les choses reçues (âsrita) et les
supports (âlambana), qui sont chacun composés de six termes, on a
dix-huit termes qu'on appelle "Dhâtus" ou contenants. La collection des six réceptacles, ce sont les organes de la vue, de l'ouïe,
de l'odorat, du goût, du toucher, et le "manas" (ou l'organe du
cœur), qui est le dernier. La collection des six choses reçues, c'est
la connaissance produite par la vue et par les autres sens jusqu'au
"manas" inclusivement. La collection des six supports, ce sont la
forme et les autres attributs sensibles jusqu'au "Dharma" (la loi ou
l'être) inclusivement.' See Burnouf, Introduction, p. 449.

Parinibbuta is again a technical term, the Sanskrit parinivrʐta
meaning 'freed from all worldly fetters,' like vimukta. See Burnouf, Introduction, p. 590. See Childers, s. v. nibbâna, p. 270,
and Notes on Dhammapada, p. 3 ; and D'Alwis, Buddhist Nirvâna,
p. 75.

CHAPTER VII.

THE VENERABLE (ARHAT).

90. There is no suffering for him who has finished his journey, and abandoned grief, who has freed himself on all sides, and thrown off all fetters.

91. They depart with their thoughts well-collected, they are not happy in their abode; like swans who have left their lake, they leave their house and home.

92. Men who have no riches, who live on recognised food, who have perceived void and unconditioned freedom (Nirvâ*n*a), their path is difficult to understand, like that of birds in the air.

---

91. Satîmanto, Sanskrit sm*ri*timanta*h*, 'possessed of memory,' but here used in the technical sense of sati, the first of the Bodhyaṅgas. See Burnouf, Introduction, p. 797. Clough translates it by 'intense thought,' and this is the original meaning of smar, even in Sanskrit. See Lectures on the Science of Language, vol. ii. p. 332.

Uyyuñ*g*anti, which Buddhaghosa explains by 'they exert themselves,' seems to me to signify in this place 'they depart,' i. e. they leave their family, and embrace an ascetic life. See note to verse 235. See also Rhys Davids, Mahâparinibbâna-sutta, Sacred Books of the East, vol. xi. p. 22.

92. Suññato and animitto are adjectives belonging to vimokho, one of the many names of Nirvâ*n*a, or, according to Childers, s. v. nibbâna, p. 270, Arhatship; see Burnouf, Introduction, pp. 442, 462, on *s*ûnya. The Sanskrit expression *s*ûnyânimittâpra*n*ihitam occurs in L'enfant egaré, 5 a, l. 4. Nimitta is cause in the most general sense, i. e. what causes existence. The commentator explains it chiefly in a moral sense : Râgâdinimittâbhâvena animitta*m*, tehi *k*a vimuttan ti animitto vimokho, i. e. owing to the absence of passion and other causes, without causation; because freed from

93. He whose appetites are stilled, who is not absorbed in enjoyment, who has perceived void and unconditioned freedom (Nirvâ*n*a), his path is difficult to understand, like that of birds in the air.

94. The gods even envy him whose senses, like horses well broken in by the driver, have been subdued, who is free from pride, and free from appetites.

95. Such a one who does his duty is tolerant like the earth, like Indra's bolt; he is like a lake without mud; no new births are in store for him.

96. His thought is quiet, quiet are his word and deed, when he has obtained freedom by true knowledge, when he has thus become a quiet man.

---

these causes, therefore it is called freedom without causation. See Childers, Pâli Dictionary, p. 270, col. 2, line 1.

The simile is intended to compare the ways of those who have obtained spiritual freedom to the flight of birds, it being difficult to understand how the birds move on without putting their feet on anything. This, at least, is the explanation of the commentator. The same metaphor occurs Mahâbh. XII, 6763. Childers translates, 'leaving no more trace of existence than a bird in the air.'

95. Without the hints given by the commentator, we should probably take the three similes of this verse in their natural sense, as illustrating the imperturbable state of an Arahanta, or venerable person. The earth is always represented as an emblem of patience; the bolt of Indra, if taken in its technical sense, as the bolt of a gate, might likewise suggest the idea of firmness; while the lake is a constant representative of serenity and purity. The commentator, however, suggests that what is meant is, that the earth, though flowers are cast on it, does not feel pleasure, nor the bolt of Indra displeasure, although less savoury things are thrown upon it; and that in like manner a wise person is indifferent to honour and dishonour.

96. That this very natural threefold division, thought, word, and deed, the trividha-dvâra or the three doors of the Buddhists (Hardy, Manual, p. 494), was not peculiar to the Buddhists or unknown to

97. The man who is free from credulity, but knows the uncreated, who has cut all ties, removed all temptations, renounced all desires, he is the greatest of men.

---

the Brahmans, has been proved against Dr. Weber by Professor Köppen in his 'Religion des Buddha,' I, p. 445. He particularly called attention to Manu XII, 4–8; and he might have added Mahâbh. XII, 4059, 6512, 6549, 6554; XIII, 5677, &c. Dr. Weber has himself afterwards brought forward a passage from the Atharva-veda, VI, 96, 3 (ya*k* *k*akshushâ manasâ ya*k* *k*a vâ*k*â upârima), which, however, has a different meaning. A better one was quoted by him from the Taitt. Ar. X, 1, 12 (yan me manasâ, vâ*k*â, karma*n*â vâ dushk*ri*ta*m* k*ri*tam). Similar expressions have been shown to exist in the Zend-avesta, and among the Manichæans (Lassen, Indische Alterthumskunde, III, p. 414; see also Boehtlingk's Dictionary, s. v. kâya, and Childers, s. v. kâyo). There was no ground, therefore, for supposing that this formula had found its way into the Christian liturgy from Persia, for, as Professor Cowell remarks (Journal of Philology, vol. vii. p. 215), Greek writers, such as Plato, employ very similar expressions, e. g. Protag. p. 348, 30, πρὸς ἅπαν ἔργον καὶ λόγον καὶ διανόημα. In fact, the opposition between words and deeds occurs in almost every writer, from Homer downwards; and the further distinction between thoughts and words is clearly implied even in such expressions as, 'they say in their heart.' That the idea of sin committed by thought was not a new idea, even to the Jews, may be seen from Prov. xxiv. 9, 'the thought of foolishness is sin.' In the Âpastamba-sûtras, lately edited by Professor Bühler, we find the expression, atho yatki*ñk*a manasâ vâ*k*â *k*akshushâ vâ sankalpayan dhyâyaty âhâbhivipa*s*yati vâ tathaiva tad bhavatîtyupadi*s*anti, 'they say that whatever a Brahman intending with his mind, voice, or eye, thinks, says, or looks, that will be.' This is clearly a very different division, and it is the same which is intended in the passage from the Atharva-veda, quoted above. In the mischief done by the eye, we have, perhaps, the first indication of the evil eye. (Mahâbh. XII, 3417. See Dhammapada, vv. 231–234.)

On the technical meaning of tâdi, see Childers, s. v. D'Alwis (p. 78) has evidently received the right interpretation, but has not understood it. Mâd*ri*sa also is used very much like tâd*ri*sa, and from it mâriso, a venerable person, in Sanskrit mârsha.

98. In a hamlet or in a forest, in the deep water or on the dry land, wherever venerable persons (Arahanta) dwell, that place is delightful.

99. Forests are delightful ; where the world finds no delight, there the passionless will find delight, for they look not for pleasures.

CHAPTER VIII.

THE THOUSANDS.

100. Even though a speech be a thousand (of words), but made up of senseless words, one word of sense is better, which if a man hears, he becomes quiet.

101. Even though a Gâthâ (poem) be a thousand (of words), but made up of senseless words, one word of a Gâthâ is better, which if a man hears, he becomes quiet.

102. Though a man recite a hundred Gâthâs made up of senseless words, one word of the law is better, which if a man hears, he becomes quiet.

103. If one man conquer in battle a thousand times thousand men, and if another conquer himself, he is the greatest of conquerors.

104, 105. One's own self conquered is better than all other people; not even a god, a Gandharva, not Mâra with Brahman could change into defeat the

---

100. This Sahasravarga, or Chapter of the Thousands, is quoted by that name in the Mahâvastu (Minayeff, Mélanges Asiatiques, VI, p. 583): Teshâm Bhagavâñ ga*s*îlânâ*m* Dharmapadeshu sahasravargam bhâshati: ‘Sahasram api vâ*k*ânâm anarthapadasa*m*hitânâm, ekârthavatî *s*reyâ yâ*m* *s*rutvâ upa*s*âmyati. Sahasram api gâthânâm anarthapadasa*m*hitânâm, ekârthavatî *s*reyâ yâ*m* *s*rutvâ upa*s*âmyati’ (MS. R. A. S. Lond.) Here the Pâli text seems decidedly more original and perfect.

104. *Gita*m, according to the commentator, stands for *g*ito (lingavipallâso, i. e. viparyâsa); see also Senart in Journal Asiatique, 1880, p. 500.

The Devas (gods), Gandharvas (fairies), and other fanciful beings of the Brahmanic religion, such as the Nâgas, Sarpas, Garu*d*as, &c.,

victory of a man who has vanquished himself, and always lives under restraint.

106. If a man for a hundred years sacrifice month after month with a thousand, and if he but for one moment pay homage to a man whose soul is grounded (in true knowledge), better is that homage than a sacrifice for a hundred years.

107. If a man for a hundred years worship Agni (fire) in the forest, and if he but for one moment pay homage to a man whose soul is grounded (in true knowledge), better is that homage than sacrifice for a hundred years.

108. Whatever a man sacrifice in this world as an offering or as an oblation for a whole year in order to gain merit, the whole of it is not worth a quarter (a farthing); reverence shown to the righteous is better.

---

were allowed to continue in the traditional language of the people who had embraced Buddhism. See the pertinent remarks of Burnouf, Introduction, pp. 134 seq., 184. On Mâra, the tempter, see v. 7. Sâstram Aiyar, On the *G*aina Religion, p. xx, says: 'Moreover as it is declared in the *G*aina Vedas that all the gods worshipped by the various Hindu sects, viz. *S*iva, Brahma, Vish*n*u, Ga*n*apati, Subramaniyan, and others, were devoted adherents of the above-mentioned Tîrthankaras, the *G*ainas therefore do not consider them as unworthy of their worship; but as they are servants of Arugan, they consider them to be deities of their system, and accordingly perform certain pû*g*âs in honour of them, and worship them also.' The case is more doubtful with orthodox Buddhists. 'Orthodox Buddhists,' as Mr. D'Alwis writes (Attanagalu-vansa, p. 55), 'do not consider the worship of the Devas as being sanctioned by him who disclaimed for himself and all the Devas any power over man's soul. Yet the Buddhists are everywhere idol-worshippers. Buddhism, however, acknowledges the existence of some of the Hindu deities, and from the various friendly offices which those Devas are said to have rendered to Gotama, Buddhists evince a respect for their idols.' See also Buddhaghosha's Parables, p. 162.

109. He who always greets and constantly reveres the aged, four things will increase to him, viz. life, beauty, happiness, power.

110. But he who lives a hundred years, vicious and unrestrained, a life of one day is better if a man is virtuous and reflecting.

111. And he who lives a hundred years, ignorant and unrestrained, a life of one day is better if a man is wise and reflecting.

112. And he who lives a hundred years, idle and weak, a life of one day is better if a man has attained firm strength.

113. And he who lives a hundred years, not seeing beginning and end, a life of one day is better if a man sees beginning and end.

114. And he who lives a hundred years, not seeing the immortal place, a life of one day is better if a man sees the immortal place.

115. And he who lives a hundred years, not seeing the highest law, a life of one day is better if a man sees the highest law.

---

109. Dr. Fausböll, in a most important note, called attention to the fact that the same verse, with slight variations, occurs in Manu. We there read, II, 121 :

Abhivâdanasîlasya nityam vriddhopasevinah,
Katvâri sampravardhante âyur vidyâ yaso balam.

Here the four things are, life, knowledge, glory, power.

In the Âpastamba-sûtras, I, 2, 5, 15, the reward promised for the same virtue is svargam âyus ka, 'heaven and long life.' It seems, therefore, as if the original idea of this verse came from the Brahmans, and was afterwards adopted by the Buddhists. How largely it spread is shown by Dr. Fausböll from the Asiatic Researches, XX, p. 259, where the same verse of the Dhammapada is mentioned as being in use among the Buddhists of Siam.

112. On kusîto, see note to verse 7.

CHAPTER IX.

EVIL.

116. If a man would hasten towards the good, he should keep his thought away from evil; if a man does what is good slothfully, his mind delights in evil.

117. If a man commits a sin, let him not do it again; let him not delight in sin: pain is the outcome of evil.

118. If a man does what is good, let him do it again; let him delight in it: happiness is the outcome of good.

119. Even an evil-doer sees happiness as long as his evil deed has not ripened; but when his evil deed has ripened, then does the evil-doer see evil.

120. Even a good man sees evil days, as long as his good deed has not ripened; but when his good deed has ripened, then does the good man see happy days.

121. Let no man think lightly of evil, saying in his heart, It will not come nigh unto me. Even by the falling of water-drops a water-pot is filled; the fool becomes full of evil, even if he gather it little by little.

122. Let no man think lightly of good, saying in his heart, It will not come nigh unto me. Even by the falling of water-drops a water-pot is filled; the wise man becomes full of good, even if he gather it little by little.

123. Let a man avoid evil deeds, as a merchant, if he has few companions and carries much wealth,

avoids a dangerous road; as a man who loves life avoids poison.

124. He who has no wound on his hand, may touch poison with his hand; poison does not affect one who has no wound; nor is there evil for one who does not commit evil.

125. If a man offend a harmless, pure, and innocent person, the evil falls back upon that fool, like light dust thrown up against the wind.

126. Some people are born again; evil-doers go to hell; righteous people go to heaven; those who are free from all worldly desires attain Nirvâna.

127. Not in the sky, not in the midst of the sea, not if we enter into the clefts of the mountains, is there known a spot in the whole world where a man might be freed from an evil deed.

128. Not in the sky, not in the midst of the sea, not if we enter into the clefts of the mountains, is there known a spot in the whole world where death could not overcome (the mortal).

---

125. Cf. Suttanipâta, v. 661; Indische Sprüche, 1582; Kathâsaritsâgara, 49, 222.

126. For a description of hell and its long, yet not endless sufferings, see Buddhaghosha's Parables, p. 132. The pleasures of heaven, too, are frequently described in these Parables and elsewhere. Buddha himself enjoyed these pleasures of heaven, before he was born for the last time. It is probably when good and evil deeds are equally balanced, that men are born again as human beings; this, at least, is the opinion of the Gainas. Cf. Chintâmani, ed. H. Bower, Introd. p. xv.

127. Cf. St. Luke xii. 2, 'For there is nothing covered that shall not be revealed;' and Psalm cxxxix. 8–12.

CHAPTER X.

PUNISHMENT.

129. All men tremble at punishment, all men fear death; remember that you are like unto them, and do not kill, nor cause slaughter.

130. All men tremble at punishment, all men love life; remember that thou art like unto them, and do not kill, nor cause slaughter.

131. He who seeking his own happiness punishes or kills beings who also long for happiness, will not find happiness after death.

---

129. One feels tempted, no doubt, to take upama in the sense of 'the nearest (der Nächste), the neighbour,' and to translate, 'having made oneself one's neighbour,' i. e. loving one's neighbour as oneself. But as upamăm, with a short a, is the correct accusative of upamâ, we must translate, 'having made oneself the likeness, the image of others, having placed oneself in the place of others.' This is an expression which occurs frequently in Sanskrit; cf. Hitopadesa I, 11:

Prânâ yathâtmano 'bhîshṭâ bhûtânâm api te tathâ,
Âtmaupamyena bhûteshu dayâm kurvanti sâdhavaḥ.

'As life is dear to oneself, it is dear also to other living beings: by comparing oneself with others, good people bestow pity on all beings.'

See also Hit. I, 12; Râm. V, 23, 5, âtmânam upamâm kṛtvâ sveshu dâreshu ramyatâm, 'making oneself a likeness, i. e. putting oneself in the position of other people, it is right to love none but one's own wife.' Dr. Fausböll has called attention to similar passages in the Mahâbhârata, XIII, 5569 seq.

130. Cf. St. Luke vi. 31.

131. Dr. Fausböll points out the striking similarity between this verse and two verses occurring in Manu and the Mahâbhârata :—

132. He who seeking his own happiness does not punish or kill beings who also long for happiness, will find happiness after death.

133. Do not speak harshly to anybody; those who are spoken to will answer thee in the same way. Angry speech is painful, blows for blows will touch thee.

134. If, like a shattered metal plate (gong), thou utter not, then thou hast reached Nirvâ*n*a; contention is not known to thee.

135. As a cowherd with his staff drives his cows into the stable, so do Age and Death drive the life of men.

136. A fool does not know when he commits his evil deeds: but the wicked man burns by his own deeds, as if burnt by fire.

137. He who inflicts pain on innocent and harmless persons, will soon come to one of these ten states:

Manu V, 45:
 Yo 'hi*m*sakâni bhûtâni hinasty âtmasukhe*kkh*ayâ,
 Sa *gî*va*m*s *k*a m*ri*ta*s k*aiva na kva*k*it sukham edhate.
Mahâbhârata XIII, 5568:
 Ahi*m*sakâni bhûtâni da*nd*ena vinihanti ya*h*,
 Âtmana*h* sukham i*kkh*an sa pretya naiva sukhî bhavet.
If it were not for ahi*m*sakâni, in which Manu and the Mahâbhârata agree, I should say that the verses in both were Sanskrit modifications of the Pâli original. The verse in the Mahâbhârata presupposes the verse of the Dhammapada.

133. See Mahâbhârata XII, 4056.

134. See Childers, s.v. nibbâna, p. 270, and s. v. kâ*m*so; D'Alwis, Buddhist Nirvâ*n*a, p. 35.

136. The metaphor of 'burning' for 'suffering' is very common in Buddhist literature. Everything burns, i. e. everything suffers, was one of the first experiences of Buddha himself. See v. 146.

138. He will have cruel suffering, loss, injury of the body, heavy affliction, or loss of mind,

139. Or a misfortune coming from the king, or a fearful accusation, or loss of relations, or destruction of treasures,

140. Or lightning-fire will burn his houses ; and when his body is destroyed, the fool will go to hell.

141. Not nakedness, not platted hair, not dirt, not fasting, or lying on the earth, not rubbing with dust,

---

138. ‘Cruel suffering’ is explained by sîsaroga, ‘headache,’ &c. ‘Loss’ is taken for loss of money. ‘Injury of the body’ is held to be the cutting off of the arm, and other limbs. ‘Heavy afflictions’ are, again, various kinds of diseases.

139. Upasarga means ‘accident, misfortune.’ Dr. Fausböll translates râgato va upassaggam by ‘fulgentis (lunae) defectionem ;’ Dr. Weber by ‘Bestrafung vom König ;’ Beal by ‘some governmental difficulty.’ Abbhakkhânam, Sanskrit abhyâkhyânam, is a heavy accusation for high treason, or similar offences. Beal translates, ‘some false accusation.’ The ‘destruction of pleasures or treasures’ is explained by gold being changed to coals (see Buddhaghosha's Parables, p. 98 ; Thiessen, Kisâgotamî, p. 6), pearls to cotton seed, corn to potsherds, and by men and cattle becoming blind, lame, &c.

141. Cf. Hibbert Lectures, p. 355. Dr. Fausböll has pointed out that the same or a very similar verse occurs in a legend taken from the Divyâvadâna, and translated by Burnouf (Introduction, p. 313 seq.) Burnouf translates the verse : ‘Ce n’est ni la coutume de marcher nu, ni les cheveux nattés, ni l’usage d’argile, ni le choix des diverses espèces d’aliments, ni l’habitude de coucher sur la terre nue, ni la poussière, ni la malpropreté, ni l’attention à fuir l’abri d’un toit, qui sont capables de dissiper le trouble dans lequel nous jettent les désirs non-satisfaits; mais qu’un homme, maître de ses sens, calme, recueilli, chaste, évitant de faire du mal à aucune créature, accomplisse la Loi, et il sera, quoique paré d’ornements, un Brâhmane, un Çramana, un Religieux.’ See also Suttanipâta, v. 248.

Walking naked and the other things mentioned in our verse are outward signs of a saintly life, and these Buddha rejects because they do not calm the passions. Nakedness he seems to have not sitting motionless, can purify a mortal who has not overcome desires.

142. He who, though dressed in fine apparel, exercises tranquillity, is quiet, subdued, restrained, chaste, and has ceased to find fault with all other beings, he indeed is a Brâhma*n*a, an ascetic (*sra*ma*n*a), a friar (bhikshu).

143. Is there in this world any man so restrained by humility that he does not mind reproof, as a well-trained horse the whip?

144. Like a well-trained horse when touched by

---

rejected on other grounds too, if we may judge from the Sumâgadhâ-avadâna: ' A number of naked friars were assembled in the house of the daughter of Anâtha-pi*nd*ika. She called her daughter-in-law, Sumâgadhâ, and said, " Go and see those highly respectable persons." Sumâgadhâ, expecting to see some of the saints, like *S*âriputra, Maudgalyâyana, and others, ran out full of joy. But when she saw these friars with their hair like pigeon wings, covered by nothing but dirt, offensive, and looking like demons, she became sad. " Why are you sad?" said her mother-in-law. Sumâgadhâ replied, "O mother, if these are saints, what must sinners be like?"'

Burnouf (Introduction, p. 312) supposed that the *G*ainas only, and not the Buddhists, allowed nakedness. But the *G*ainas, too, do not allow it universally. They are divided into two parties, the *S*vetambaras and Digambaras. The *S*vetambaras, clad in white, are the followers of Par*s*vanâtha, and wear clothes. The Digambaras, i. e. sky-clad, disrobed, are followers of Mahâvîra, resident chiefly in Southern India. At present they, too, wear clothing, but not when eating. See Sâstram Aiyar, p. xxi.

The *g*a*t*â, or the hair platted and gathered up in a knot, was a sign of a *S*aiva ascetic. The sitting motionless is one of the postures assumed by ascetics. Clough explains ukku*t*ika as 'the act of sitting on the heels;' Wilson gives for utka*t*ukâsana, 'sitting on the hams.' See Fausböll, note on verse 140.

142. As to da*nd*anidhâna, see Mahâbh. XII, 6559, and Sutta-nipâta, v. 34.

143, 144. I am very doubtful as to the real meaning of these verses. If their object is to show how reproof or punishment

the whip, be ye active and lively, and by faith, by
virtue, by energy, by meditation, by discernment of
the law you will overcome this great pain (of reproof),
perfect in knowledge and in behaviour, and never
forgetful.

145. Well-makers lead the water (wherever they
like); fletchers bend the arrow; carpenters bend
a log of wood; good people fashion themselves.

---

should be borne, my translation would be right, though alpabodhati
in the sense of parvi facere is strange.

145. The same as verse 80. According to Fausböll and Subhûti
we ought to render the verses by, 'What man is there found on
earth so restrained by shame that he never provokes reproof, as a
good horse the whip?'   See Childers, s. v. appabodhati.

CHAPTER XI.

OLD AGE.

146. How is there laughter, how is there joy, as this world is always burning? Why do you not seek a light, ye who are surrounded by darkness?

147. Look at this dressed-up lump, covered with wounds, joined together, sickly, full of many thoughts, which has no strength, no hold!

148. This body is wasted, full of sickness, and frail; this heap of corruption breaks to pieces, life indeed ends in death.

---

148. Dr. Fausböll informs me that Childers proposed the emendation mara*n*anta*m* hi g*î*vita*m*. The following extract from a letter, addressed by Childers to Dr. Fausböll, will be read with interest :— 'As regards Dhp. v. 148, I have no doubt whatever. I quite agree with you that the idea (mors est vita ejus) is a profound and noble one, but the question is, Is the idea there? I think not. Mara*n*a*m* tamhi g*î*vita*m* is not Pâli, I mean not a Pâli construction, and years ago even it grated on my ear as a harsh phrase. The reading of your MSS. of the texts is nothing; your MSS. of Dhammapada are very bad ones, and it is merely the vicious Sinhalese spelling of bad MSS., like kamma*m*ta*m* for kammanta*m*. But the comment sets the question at rest at once, for it explains mara*n*anta*m* by mara*n*a-pariyosâna*m*, which is exactly the same. I see there is one serious difficulty left, that all your MSS. seem to have tamhi, and not ta*m* hi; but are you sure it is so? There was a Dhammapada in the India Office Library, and I had a great hunt for it a few days ago, but to my deep disappointment it is missing. I do not agree with you that the sentence "All Life is bounded by Death," is trivial: it is a truism, but half the noblest passages in poetry are truisms, and unless I greatly mistake, this very passage will be found in many other literatures.'

Dr. Fausböll adds :—

'I have still the same doubt as before, because of all my

[10]   g

149. Those white bones, like gourds thrown away in the autumn, what pleasure is there in looking at them?

150. After a stronghold has been made of the bones, it is covered with flesh and blood, and there dwell in it old age and death, pride and deceit.

151. The brilliant chariots of kings are destroyed, the body also approaches destruction, but the virtue of good people never approaches destruction,—thus do the good say to the good.

152. A man who has learnt little, grows old like an ox; his flesh grows, but his knowledge does not grow.

153, 154. Looking for the maker of this tabernacle, I shall have to run through a course of many births, so long as I do not find (him); and painful is birth again and again. But now, maker of the tabernacle, thou hast been seen; thou shalt not make up

---

MSS. reading mara*nam* tamhi. I do not know the readings of the London MSS. The explanation of the commentary does not settle the question, as it may as well be considered an explanation of my reading as of the reading which Childers proposed.—V. FAUSBÖLL.'

149. In the Rudrâya*n*âvadâna of the Divyâvadâna this verse appears as,

Yânîmâny apariddhâni vikshiptâni di*s*o di*s*a*h*,
Kapotavar*n*ány asthîni tâni d*ri*sh*t*vaiha kâ rati*h*.

See Schiefner, Mél. Asiat. VIII, p. 589; *G*âtaka, vol. i. p. 322.

150. The expression ma*m*salohitalepanam is curiously like the expression used in Manu VI, 76, mâ*m*sa*s*o*n*italepanam, and in several passages of the Mahâbhârata, XII, 12462, 12053, as pointed out by Dr. Fausböll.

153, 154. These two verses are famous among Buddhists, for they are the words which the founder of Buddhism is supposed to have uttered at the moment he attained to Buddhahood. (See Spence Hardy, Manual, p. 180.) According to the Lalita-vistara, however, the words uttered on that solemn occasion were those this tabernacle again. All thy rafters are broken, thy ridge-pole is sundered; the mind, approaching the Eternal (visankhâra, nirvâ*n*a), has attained to the extinction of all desires.

---

quoted in the note to verse 39. In the commentary on the Brahma*g*âla this verse is called the first speech of Buddha, his last speech being the words in the Mahâparinibbâna-sutta, 'Life is subject to age; strive in earnest.' The words used in the Mahâparinibbâna-sutta, Chap. IV, 2, *K*atunna*m* dhammânam ananubodhâ appa*ri*vedhâ evam ida*m* digham addhânam sandhâvita*m* sa*m*sârita*m* mama*ñ* *k*' eva tumhâka*ñ* *k*a, answer to the anticipation expressed in our verse.

The exact rendering of this verse has been much discussed, chiefly by Mr. D'Alwis in the Attanugaluvansa, p. cxxviii, and again in his Buddhist Nirvâ*n*a, p. 78; also by Childers, Notes on Dhammapada, p. 4, and in his Dictionary. Gogerly translated: 'Through various transmigrations I must travel, if I do not discover the builder whom I seek.' Spence Hardy: 'Through many different births I have run (to me not having found), seeking the architect of the desire-resembling house.' Fausböll: 'Multiplices generationis revolutiones percurreram, non inveniens, domus (corporis) fabricatorem quaerens.' And again (p. 322): 'Multarum generationum revolutio mihi subeunda esset, nisi invenissem domus fabricatorem.' Childers: 'I have run through the revolution of countless births, seeking the architect of this dwelling and finding him not.' D'Alwis: 'Through transmigrations of numerous births have I run, not discovering, (though) seeking the house-builder.' All depends on how we take sandhavissam, which Fausböll takes as a conditional, Childers, following Trenckner, as an aorist, because the sense imperatively requires an aorist. In either case, the dropping of the augment and the doubling of the s are, however, irregular. Sandhavissam is the regular form of the future, and as such I translate it, qualifying, however, the future, by the participle present anibbisan, i. e. not finding, and taking it in the sense of, if or so long as I do not find the true cause of existence. I had formerly translated anibbisan, as not resting (anirvi*s*an), but the commentator seems to authorise the meaning of not finding (avindanto, alabhanto), and in that case all the material difficulties of the verse seem to me to disappear.

'The maker of the tabernacle' is explained as a poetical expression for the cause of new births, at least according to the views of

155. Men who have not observed proper discipline, and have not gained treasure in their youth, perish like old herons in a lake without fish.

156. Men who have not observed proper discipline, and have not gained treasure in their youth, lie, like broken bows, sighing after the past.

Buddha's followers, whatever his own views may have been. Buddha had conquered Mâra, the representative of worldly temptations, the father of worldly desires, and as desires (tamhâ) are, by means of upâdâna and bhava, the cause of gâti, or 'birth,' the destruction of desires and the conquest of Mâra are nearly the same thing, though expressed differently in the philosophical and legendary language of the Buddhists. Tamhâ, 'thirst' or 'desire,' is mentioned as serving in the army of Mâra. (Lotus, p. 443.)

155. On ghâyanti, i. e. kshâyanti, see Dr. Bollensen's learned remarks, Zeitschrift der Deutschen Morgenl. Gesellschaft, XVIII, 834, and Boehtlingk-Roth, s. v. kshâ.

CHAPTER XII.

SELF.

157. If a man hold himself dear, let him watch himself carefully; during one at least out of the three watches a wise man should be watchful.

158. Let each man direct himself first to what is proper, then let him teach others; thus a wise man will not suffer.

159. If a man make himself as he teaches others to be, then, being himself well subdued, he may subdue (others); one's own self is indeed difficult to subdue.

160. Self is the lord of self, who else could be the lord? With self well subdued, a man finds a lord such as few can find.

161. The evil done by oneself, self-begotten, self-bred, crushes the foolish, as a diamond breaks a precious stone.

162. He whose wickedness is very great brings himself down to that state where his enemy wishes him to be, as a creeper does with the tree which it surrounds.

163. Bad deeds, and deeds hurtful to ourselves, are easy to do; what is beneficial and good, that is very difficult to do.

---

157. The three watches of the night are meant for the three stages of life. Cf. St. Mark xiii. 37, 'And what I say unto you, I say unto all, Watch.'

158. Cf. *G*âtaka, vol. ii. p. 441.

161. The Chinese translation renders va*g*iram by 'steel drill.'

164. The foolish man who scorns the rule of the venerable (Arahat), of the elect (Ariya), of the virtuous, and follows false doctrine, he bears fruit to his own destruction, like the fruits of the Ka*tth*aka reed.

165. By oneself the evil is done, by oneself one suffers; by oneself evil is left undone, by oneself one is purified. Purity and impurity belong to oneself, no one can purify another.

166. Let no one forget his own duty for the sake of another's, however great; let a man, after he has discerned his own duty, be always attentive to his duty.

---

164. The reed either dies after it has borne fruit, or is cut down for the sake of its fruit.

Di*tth*i, literally 'view,' is used even by itself, like the Greek 'hairesis,' in the sense of heresy (see Burnouf, Lotus, p. 444). In other places a distinction is made between mi*kkh*âdi*tth*i (vv. 167, 316) and sammâdi*tth*i (v. 319). If arahata*m* ariyâna*m* are used in their technical sense, we should translate 'the reverend Arhats,'— Arhat being the highest degree of the four orders of Ariyas, viz. Srotaâpanna, Sakadâgâmin, Anâgâmin, and Arhat. See note to verse 178.

166. Attha, lit. 'object,' must here be taken in a moral sense, as 'duty' rather than as 'advantage.' Childers rendered it by 'spiritual good.' The story which Buddhaghosa tells of the Thera Attadattha gives a clue to the origin of some of his parables, which seem to have been invented to suit the text of the Dhammapada rather than vice versâ. A similar case occurs in the commentary to verse 227.

CHAPTER XIII.

THE WORLD.

167. Do not follow the evil law! Do not live on in thoughtlessness! Do not follow false doctrine! Be not a friend of the world.

168. Rouse thyself! do not be idle! Follow the law of virtue! The virtuous rests in bliss in this world and in the next.

169. Follow the law of virtue; do not follow that of sin. The virtuous rests in bliss in this world and in the next.

170. Look upon the world as a bubble, look upon it as a mirage: the king of death does not see him who thus looks down upon the world.

171. Come, look at this glittering world, like unto a royal chariot; the foolish are immersed in it, but the wise do not touch it.

172. He who formerly was reckless and afterwards became sober, brightens up this world, like the moon when freed from clouds.

173. He whose evil deeds are covered by good deeds, brightens up this world, like the moon when freed from clouds.

174. This world is dark, few only can see here; a few only go to heaven, like birds escaped from the net.

175. The swans go on the path of the sun, they go through the ether by means of their miraculous

168, 169. See Rhys Davids, Buddhism, p. 65.

170. See Suttanipâta, v. 1118.

175. Hamsa may be meant for the bird, whether flamingo, or swan, or ibis (see Hardy, Manual, p. 17), but it may also, I believe,

power; the wise are led out of this world, when they have conquered Mâra and his train.

176. If a man has transgressed one law, and speaks lies, and scoffs at another world, there is no evil he will not do.

177. The uncharitable do not go to the world of the gods; fools only do not praise liberality; a wise man rejoices in liberality, and through it becomes blessed in the other world.

178. Better than sovereignty over the earth, better than going to heaven, better than lordship over all worlds, is the reward of the first step in holiness.

---

be taken in the sense of saint. As to iddhi, 'magical power,' i.e. *ri*ddhi, see Burnouf, Lotus, p. 310; Spence Hardy, Manual, pp. 498, 504; Legends, pp. 55, 177; and note to verse 254.

178. Sotâpatti, the technical term for the first step in the path that leads to Nirvâna. There are four such steps, or stages, and on entering each, a man receives a new title :—

(1) The *S*rotaâpanna, lit. he who has got into the stream. A man may have seven more births before he reaches the other shore, i. e. Nirvâna.

(2) Sak*ri*dâgâmin, lit. he who comes back once, so called because, after having entered this stage, a man is born only once more among men or gods. Childers shows that this involves really two more births, one in the deva world, the other in the world of men. Burnouf says the same, Introduction, p. 293.

(3) Anâgâmin, lit. he who does not come back, so called because, after this stage, a man cannot be born again in a lower world, but can only be born into a Brahman world, before he reaches Nirvâna.

(4) Arhat, the venerable, the perfect, who has reached the highest stage that can be reached, and from which Nirvâna is perceived (sukkhavipassanâ, Lotus, p. 849). See Hardy, Eastern Monachism, p. 280; Burnouf, Introduction, p. 209; Köppen, p. 398; D'Alwis, Attanugaluvansa, p. cxxiv; Feer, Sutra en 42 articles, p. 6.

CHAPTER XIV.

THE BUDDHA (THE AWAKENED).

179. He whose conquest is not conquered again, into whose conquest no one in this world enters, by what track can you lead him, the Awakened, the Omniscient, the trackless?

180. He whom no desire with its snares and poisons can lead astray, by what track can you lead him, the Awakened, the Omniscient, the trackless?

181. Even the gods envy those who are awakened and not forgetful, who are given to meditation, who are wise, and who delight in the repose of retirement (from the world).

182. Difficult (to obtain) is the conception of men, difficult is the life of mortals, difficult is the hearing of the True Law, difficult is the birth of the Awakened (the attainment of Buddhahood).

179, 180. Buddha, the Awakened, is to be taken as an appellative rather than as the proper name of the Buddha (see v. 183). It means, anybody who has arrived at complete knowledge. Anantago*k*aram I take in the sense of, possessed of unlimited knowledge. Apadam, which Dr. Fausböll takes as an epithet of Buddha and translates by 'non investigabilis,' is translated 'trackless,' in order to show the play on the word pada; see Childers, s. v. The commentator says: 'The man who is possessed of even a single one of such conditions as râga, &c., him ye may lead forward; but the Buddha has not even one condition or basis of renewed existence, and therefore by what track will you lead this unconditioned Buddha?' Cf. Dhp. vv. 92, 420; and *G*âtaka, vol. i. pp. 79, 313.

182. Mr. Beal (Dhammapada, p. 110) states that this verse occurs in the Sûtra of the Forty-two Sections.

183. Not to commit any sin, to do good, and to purify one's mind, that is the teaching of (all) the Awakened.

184. The Awakened call patience the highest penance, long-suffering the highest Nirvâ*n*a; for he is not an anchorite (pravra*g*ita) who strikes others, he is not an ascetic (*s*rama*n*a) who insults others.

185. Not to blame, not to strike, to live restrained under the law, to be moderate in eating, to sleep and sit alone, and to dwell on the highest thoughts,— this is the teaching of the Awakened.

---

183. This verse is again one of the most solemn verses among the Buddhists. According to Csoma Körösi, it ought to follow the famous Âryâ stanza, ' Ye dhammâ' (Lotus, p. 522), and serve as its complement. But though this may be the case in Tibet, it was not so originally. The same verse (ascribed to Kanakamuni) occurs at the end of the Chinese translation of the Prâtimoksha (Beal, J. R. A. S. XIX, p. 473; Catena, p. 159); in the Tibetan translation of the Gâthâsaṅgraha, v. 14 (Schiefner, Mél. Asiat. VIII, pp. 568, 586; and Csoma Körösi, As. Res. XX, p. 79). Burnouf has fully discussed the metre and meaning of our verse on pp. 527, 528 of his ' Lotus.' He prefers sa*k*ittaparidamanam, which Csoma translated by ' the mind must be brought under entire subjection' (sva*k*ittaparidamanam), and the late Dr. Mill by ' proprii intellectus subjugatio.' But his own MS. of the Mahâpadhâna-sutta gave likewise sa*k*ittapariyodapanam, and this is no doubt the correct reading. (See D'Alwis, Attanugaluvansa, p. cxxix.) We found pariyodappeya in verse 88, in the sense of purging oneself from the troubles of thought. From the same verb, (pari) ava + dai, we may derive the name Avadâna, a legend, originally a pure and virtuous act, an ἀρίστεια, afterwards a sacred story, and possibly a story the hearing of which purifies the mind. See Boehtlingk-Roth, s. v. avadâna.

184. Childers, following the commentator, translates, ' Patience, which is long-suffering, is the best devotion, the Buddhas declare that Nirvâ*n*a is the best (of things).'

185. Cf. Suttanipâta, v. 337. Pâtimokkhe, ' under the law,' i. e. according to the law, the law which leads to Moksha, or ' freedom.' Prâtimoksha is the title of the oldest collection of the moral laws

186. There is no satisfying lusts, even by a shower
of gold pieces; he who knows that lusts have a short
taste and cause pain, he is wise;

187. Even in heavenly pleasures he finds no satisfaction, the disciple who is fully awakened delights
only in the destruction of all desires.

188. Men, driven by fear, go to many a refuge, to
mountains and forests, to groves and sacred trees.

189. But that is not a safe refuge, that is not the
best refuge; a man is not delivered from all pains
after having gone to that refuge.

190. He who takes refuge with Buddha, the Law,

---

of the Buddhists (Burnouf, Introduction, p. 300; Bigandet, The
Life of Gaudama, p. 439; Rhys Davids, Buddhism, p. 162), and as
it was common both to the Southern and the Northern Buddhists,
pâtimokkhe in our passage may possibly be meant, as Professor
Weber suggests, as the title of that very collection. The commentator explains it by *getthakasîla* and pâtimokkhasîla. Sayanâsam
might stand for *sayanâsanam*, see Mahâbh. XII, 6684; but in Buddhist literature it is intended for *sayanâsanam*; see also Mahâbh. XII,
9978, *sayyâsane*. Fausböll now reads pânta instead of patthañ.

187. There is a curious similarity between this verse and verse
6503 (9919) of the *Sântiparva* :

 Ya*k ka* kâmasukha*m* loke, ya*k ka* divyam mahat sukham,
 T*ri*shnâkshayasukhasyaite nârhata*h* shoda*sî*m kalâm.

'And whatever delight of love there is on earth, and whatever is
the great delight in heaven, they are not worth the sixteenth part
of the pleasure which springs from the destruction of all desires.'
The two verses 186, 187 are ascribed to king Mandhât*ri*, shortly
before his death (Mél. Asiat.VIII, p. 471; see also *G*âtaka, vol. ii.
p. 113).

188–192. These verses occur in Sanskrit in the Prâtihâryasûtra,
translated by Burnouf, Introduction, pp. 162–189; see p. 186.
Burnouf translates rukkha*k*etyâni by 'arbres consacrés ;' properly,
sacred shrines under or near a tree. See also *G*âtaka, vol. i. p. 97.

190. Buddha, Dharma, and Saṅgha are called the Tri*s*ara*n*a
(cf. Burnouf, Introd. p. 630). The four holy truths are the four
statements that there is pain in this world, that the source of

and the Church ; he who, with clear understanding, sees the four holy truths :—

191. Viz. pain, the origin of pain, the destruction of pain, and the eightfold holy way that leads to the quieting of pain ;—

192. That is the safe refuge, that is the best refuge ; having gone to that refuge, a man is delivered from all pain.

193. A supernatural person (a Buddha) is not easily found, he is not born everywhere. Wherever such a sage is born, that race prospers.

194. Happy is the arising of the awakened, happy is the teaching of the True Law, happy is peace in the church, happy is the devotion of those who are at peace.

195, 196. He who pays homage to those who deserve homage, whether the awakened (Buddha) or their disciples, those who have overcome the host (of evils), and crossed the flood of sorrow, he who pays homage to such as have found deliverance and know no fear, his merit can never be measured by anybody.

---

pain is desire, that desire can be annihilated, that there is a way (shown by Buddha) by which the annihilation of all desires can be achieved, and freedom be obtained. That way consists of eight parts. (See Burnouf, Introduction, p. 630.) The eightfold way forms the subject of Chapter XVIII. (See also Feer, Journal As. 1870, p. 418, and Chips from a German Workshop, 2nd ed. vol. i. p. 251 seq.)

CHAPTER XV.

HAPPINESS.

197. Let us live happily then, not hating those who hate us! among men who hate us let us dwell free from hatred!

198. Let us live happily then, free from ailments among the ailing! among men who are ailing let us dwell free from ailments!

199. Let us live happily then, free from greed among the greedy! among men who are greedy let us dwell free from greed!

200. Let us live happily then, though we call nothing our own! We shall be like the bright gods, feeding on happiness!

201. Victory breeds hatred, for the conquered is unhappy. He who has given up both victory and defeat, he, the contented, is happy.

---

198. The ailment here meant is moral rather than physical. Cf. Mahâbh. XII, 9924, *samprasânto nirâmayaḥ*; 9925, *yo 'sau prânântiko rogas tâm trishnâm tyagataḥ sukham.*

200. The words placed in the mouth of the king of Videha, while his residence Mithilâ was in flames, are curiously like our verse; cf. Mahâbh. XII, 9917,

> Susukham vata gîvâmi yasya me nâsti kiñkana,
> Mithilâyâm pradîptâyâm na me dahyati kiñkana.

'I live happily, indeed, for I have nothing; while Mithilâ is in flames, nothing of mine is burning.' Cf. Muir, Religious Sentiments, p. 106.

The âbhassara, i.e. âbhâsvara, 'the bright gods,' are frequently mentioned. Cf. Burnouf, Introd. p. 611.

201. This verse is ascribed to Buddha, when he heard of the defeat of Agâtasatru by Prasenagit. It exists in the Northern or

202. There is no fire like passion; there is no losing throw like hatred; there is no pain like this body; there is no happiness higher than rest.

203. Hunger is the worst of diseases, the body the greatest of pains; if one knows this truly, that is Nirvâ*n*a, the highest happiness.

Sanskrit and in the Southern or Pâli texts, i. e. in the Avadâna-*s*ataka, in the Sa*m*yutta-nikâya. See Feer, Comptes Rendus, 1871, p. 44, and Journal As. 1880, p. 509.   In the Avadâna-*s*ataka, the Sanskrit version is—

> *G*ayo vairam prasavati, du*h*kha*m* *s*ete parâ*g*ita*h*
> Upa*s*ânta*h* sukha*m* *s*ete hitvâ *g*ayaparâ*g*ayam.

202. I take kali in the sense of an unlucky die which makes a player lose his game.   A real simile seems wanted here, as in verse 251, where, for the same reason, I translate graha by 'shark,' not by 'captivitas,' as Dr. Fausböll proposes.   The same scholar translates kali in our verse by 'peccatum.'   If there is any objection to translating kali in Pâli by 'unlucky die,' I should still prefer to take it in the sense of the age of depravity, or the demon of depravity.   To judge from Abhidhânappadîpikâ, 1106, kali was used for parâ*g*aya, i. e. loss at game, a losing throw, and occurs in that sense again in verse 252.   The Chinese translation has, 'there is no distress (poison) worse than hate.'   A similar verse occurs Mahâbh. *S*ântip. 175, v. 35.

'Body' for khandha is a free translation, but it is difficult to find any other rendering.   The Chinese translation also has 'body.' According to the Buddhists each sentient being consists of five khandhas (skandha), or aggregates, the organized body (rûpa-khandha) with its four internal capacities of sensation (vedanâ), perception (sa*ñ*g*ñ*â), conception (sa*m*skâra), knowledge (vi*g*ñâna). See Burnouf, Introd. pp. 589, 634; Lotus, p. 335.

203. Sa*m*skâra is the fourth of the five khandhas, but the commentator takes it here, as well as in verse 255, for the five khandhas together, in which case we can only translate it by 'body.'   See also verse 278.   Childers proposes 'organic life' (Notes on Dhammapada, p. 1).   There is, however, another sa*m*skâra, that which follows immediately upon avidyâ, 'ignorance,' as the second of the nidânas, or 'causes of existence,' and this too might be called the greatest pain, considering that it is the cause of birth, which is the cause of all pain.   Sa*m*skâra seems sometimes to have a different

204. Health is the greatest of gifts, contentedness the best riches; trust is the best of relationships, Nirvâ*n*a the highest happiness.

205. He who has tasted the sweetness of solitude and tranquillity, is free from fear and free from sin, while he tastes the sweetness of drinking in the law.

206. The sight of the elect (Arya) is good, to live with them is always happiness; if a man does not see fools, he will be truly happy.

207. He who walks in the company of fools suffers a long way; company with fools, as with an enemy, is always painful; company with the wise is pleasure, like meeting with kinsfolk.

V

208. Therefore, one ought to follow the wise, the intelligent, the learned, the much enduring, the dutiful, the elect; one ought to follow a good and wise man, as the moon follows the path of the stars.

and less technical meaning, being used in the sense of conceptions, plans, desires, as, for instance, in verse 368, where sankhârânam khayam is used much like ta*m*hâkhaya. Again, in his comment on verse 75, Buddhaghosa says, upadhiviveko sankhârasanga*n*ika*m* vinodeti; and again, upadhiviveko *k*a nirupadhînâ*m* puggalâna*m* visankhâragatânâm.

For a similar sentiment, see Stanislas Julien, Les Avadânas, vol. i. p. 40, 'Le corps est la plus grande source de souffrance,' &c. I should say that the khandhas in verse 202 and the sankhâras in verse 203 are nearly, if not quite, synonymous. I should prefer to read *g*iga*kkh*â-paramâ as a compound. *G*iga*kkh*â, or as it is written in one MS., diga*kkh*â (Sk. *g*ighatsâ), means not only ' hunger,' but ' appetite, desire.'

204. Childers translates, 'the best kinsman is a man you can trust.'

205. Cf. Suttanipâta, v. 256.

208. I should like to read sukho *k*a dhîrasa*m*vâso.

CHAPTER XVI.

PLEASURE.

209. He who gives himself to vanity, and does not give himself to meditation, forgetting the real aim (of life) and grasping at pleasure, will in time envy him who has exerted himself in meditation.

210. Let no man ever look for what is pleasant, or what is unpleasant. Not to see what is pleasant is pain, and it is pain to see what is unpleasant.

211. Let, therefore, no man love anything; loss of the beloved is evil. Those who love nothing, and hate nothing, have no fetters.

212. From pleasure comes grief, from pleasure comes fear; he who is free from pleasure knows neither grief nor fear.

213. From affection comes grief, from affection comes fear; he who is free from affection knows neither grief nor fear.

214. From lust comes grief, from lust comes fear; he who is free from lust knows neither grief nor fear.

215. From love comes grief, from love comes fear; he who is free from love knows neither grief nor fear.

216. From greed comes grief, from greed comes fear; he who is free from greed knows neither grief nor fear.

217. He who possesses virtue and intelligence,

214. See Beal, Catena, p. 200.

who is just, speaks the truth, and does what is his own business, him the world will hold dear.

218. He in whom a desire for the Ineffable (Nirvâ*n*a) has sprung up, who is satisfied in his mind, and whose thoughts are not bewildered by love, he is called ûrdhva*m*srotas (carried upwards by the stream).

219. Kinsmen, friends, and lovers salute a man who has been long away, and returns safe from afar.

220. In like manner his good works receive him who has done good, and has gone from this world to the other ;—as kinsmen receive a friend on his return.

---

218. Ûrdhva*m*srotas or uddha*m*soto is the technical name for one who has reached the world of the Av*ri*has (Aviha), and is proceeding to that of the Akanish*t*has (Akani*tt*ha). This is the last stage before he reaches the formless world, the Arûpadhâtu. (See Buddhaghosha's Parables, p. 123; Burnouf, Introduction, p. 599.) Originally ûrdhva*m*srotas may have been used in a less technical sense, meaning one who swims against the stream, and is not carried away by the vulgar passions of the world.

CHAPTER XVII.

ANGER.

221. Let a man leave anger, let him forsake pride, let him overcome all bondage! No sufferings befall the man who is not attached to name and form, and who calls nothing his own.

222. He who holds back rising anger like a rolling chariot, him I call a real driver; other people are but holding the reins.

223. Let a man overcome anger by love, let him overcome evil by good; let him overcome the greedy by liberality, the liar by truth!

224. Speak the truth, do not yield to anger; give, if thou art asked for little; by these three steps thou wilt go near the gods.

225. The sages who injure nobody, and who always control their body, they will go to the unchangeable place (Nirvâna), where, if they have gone, they will suffer no more.

226. Those who are ever watchful, who study day and night, and who strive after Nirvâna, their passions will come to an end.

227. This is an old saying, O Atula, this is not only of to-day: 'They blame him who sits silent,

---

221. 'Name and form' or 'mind and body' is the translation of nâma-rûpa, the ninth of the Buddhist Nidânas. Cf. Burnouf, Introduction, p. 501; see also Gogerly, Lecture on Buddhism, and Bigandet, The Life of Gaudama, p. 454.

223. Mahâbh. XII, 3550, asâdhum sadhunâ gayet. Cf. Ten Gâtakas, ed. Fausböll, p. 5.

227. It appears from the commentary that porânam and aggatanam are neuters, referring to what happened formerly and what

they blame him who speaks much, they also blame him who says little ; there is no one on earth who is not blamed.

228. There never was, there never will be, nor is there now, a man who is always blamed, or a man who is always praised.

229, 230. But he whom those who discriminate praise continually day after day, as without blemish, wise, rich in knowledge and virtue, who would dare to blame him, like a coin made of gold from the Gambû river? Even the gods praise him, he is praised even by Brahman.

231. Beware of bodily anger, and control thy body! Leave the sins of the body, and with thy body practise virtue!

232. Beware of the anger of the tongue, and control thy tongue! Leave the sins of the tongue, and practise virtue with thy tongue!

233. Beware of the anger of the mind, and control thy mind! Leave the sins of the mind, and practise virtue with thy mind!

234. The wise who control their body, who control their tongue, the wise who control their mind, are indeed well controlled.

happens to-day, and that they are not to be taken as adjectives referring to âsînam, &c. The commentator must have read atula instead of atulam, and he explains it as the name of a pupil whom Gautama addressed by that name. This may be so (see note to verse 166); but atula may also be taken in the sense of incomparable (Mahâbh. XIII, 1937), and in that case we ought to supply, with Professor Weber, some such word as ‘saw’ or ‘saying.’

230. The Brahman worlds are higher that the Deva worlds as the Brahman is higher than a Deva; see Hardy, Manual, p. 25; Burnouf, Introduction, pp. 134, 184.

CHAPTER XVIII.

IMPURITY.

235. Thou art now like a sear leaf, the messengers of death (Yama) have come near to thee; thou standest at the door of thy departure, and thou hast no provision for thy journey.

236. Make thyself an island, work hard, be wise! When thy impurities are blown away, and thou art free from guilt, thou wilt enter into the heavenly world of the elect (Ariya).

237. Thy life has come to an end, thou art come near to death (Yama), there is no resting-place for thee on the road, and thou hast no provision for thy journey.

238. Make thyself an island, work hard, be wise! When thy impurities are blown away, and thou art free from guilt, thou wilt not enter again into birth and decay.

239. Let a wise man blow off the impurities of his self, as a smith blows off the impurities of silver, one by one, little by little, and from time to time.

240. As the impurity which springs from the iron,

---

235. Uyyoga seems to mean departure. See Buddhaghosa's commentary on verse 152, p. 319, l. 1; Fausböll, Five *G*âtakas, p. 35.

236. 'An island,' for a drowning man to save himself; (see verse 25.) Dîpankara is the name of one of the former Buddhas, and it is also used as an appellative of the Buddha, but is always derived from dîpo, 'a lamp.'

239. This verse is the foundation of the thirty-fourth section of the Sûtra of the forty-two sections; see Beal, Catena, p. 201; Suttanipâta, v. 962.

when it springs from it, destroys it ; thus do a transgressor's own works lead him to the evil path.

241. The taint of prayers is non-repetition ; the taint of houses, non-repair ; the taint of the body is sloth ; the taint of a watchman, thoughtlessness.

242. Bad conduct is the taint of woman, greediness the taint of a benefactor; tainted are all evil ways, in this world and in the next.

243. But there is a taint worse than all taints,— ignorance is the greatest taint. O mendicants ! throw off that taint, and become taintless !

244. Life is easy to live for a man who is without shame, a crow hero, a mischief-maker, an insulting, bold, and wretched fellow.

245. But life is hard to live for a modest man, who always looks for what is pure, who is disinterested, quiet, spotless, and intelligent.

246. He who destroys life, who speaks untruth, who in this world takes what is not given him, who goes to another man's wife ;

247. And the man who gives himself to drinking intoxicating liquors, he, even in this world, digs up his own root.

248. O man, know this, that the unrestrained are in a bad state ; take care that greediness and vice do not bring thee to grief for a long time !

244. Pakkhandin is identified by Dr. Fausböll with praskandin, one who jumps forward, insults, or, as Buddhaghosa explains it, one who meddles with other people's business, an interloper. At all events, it is a term of reproach, and, as it would seem, of theological reproach.

246. On the five principal commandments which are recapitulated in verses 246 and 247, see Buddhaghosha's Parables, p. 153.

248. Cf. Mahâbhârata XII, 4055, yeshâm vrittis ka samyatâ. See also verse 307.

249. The world gives according to their faith or according to their pleasure : if a man frets about the food and the drink given to others, he will find no rest either by day or by night.

250. He in whom that feeling is destroyed, and taken out with the very root, finds rest by day and by night.

251. There is no fire like passion, there is no shark like hatred, there is no snare like folly, there is no torrent like greed.

252. The fault of others is easily perceived, but that of oneself is difficult to perceive ; a man winnows his neighbour's faults like chaff, but his own fault he hides, as a cheat hides the bad die from the gambler.

253. If a man looks after the faults of others, and is always inclined to be offended, his own passions will grow, and he is far from the destruction of passions.

254. There is no path through the air, a man is not a Samana by outward acts.   The world

---

249. This verse has evidently regard to the feelings of the Bhikshus or mendicants who receive either much or little, and who are exhorted not to be envious if others receive more than they themselves.   Several of the Parables illustrate this feeling.

251. Dr. Fausböll translates gaho by ‘ captivitas,’ Dr. Weber by ‘ fetter.’ I take it in the same sense as grâha in Manu VI, 78; and Buddhaghosa does the same, though he assigns to grâha a more general meaning, viz. anything that seizes, whether an evil spirit (yakkha), a serpent (agagara), or a crocodile (kumbhîla).

Greed or thirst is represented as a river in Lalita-vistara, ed. Calc. p. 482, trishnâ-nadî tivegâ prasoshitâ me gñânasûryena, ‘ the wild river of thirst is dried up by the sun of my knowledge.’

252. See Childers, Notes, p. 7; St. Matthew vii. 3.

253. As to âsava, ‘ appetite, passion,’ see note to verse 39.

254. I have translated this verse very freely, and not in accord-

delights in vanity, the Tathâgatas (the Buddhas) are free from vanity.

255. There is no path through the air, a man is not a Samana by outward acts. No creatures are eternal; but the awakened (Buddha) are never shaken.

---

ance with Buddhaghosa's commentary. Dr. Fausböll proposed to translate, 'No one who is outside the Buddhist community can walk through the air, but only a Samana;' and the same view is taken by Professor Weber, though he arrives at it by a different construction. Now it is perfectly true that the idea of magical powers (riddhi) which enable saints to walk through the air, &c., occurs in the Dhammapada, see v. 175, note. But the Dhammapada may contain earlier and later verses, and in that case our verse might be an early protest on the part of Buddha against the belief in such miraculous powers. We know how Buddha himself protested against his disciples being called upon to perform vulgar miracles. 'I command my disciples not to work miracles,' he said, 'but to hide their good deeds, and to show their sins' (Burnouf, Introd. p. 170). It would be in harmony with this sentiment if we translated our verse as I have done. As to bahira, I should take it in the sense of 'external,' as opposed to adhyâtmika, or 'internal;' and the meaning would be, 'a Samana is not a Samana by outward acts, but by his heart.' D'Alwis translates (p. 85): 'There is no footprint in the air; there is not a Samana out of the pale of the Buddhist community.'

Prapañka, which I have here translated by 'vanity,' seems to include the whole host of human weaknesses; cf. v. 196, where it is explained by tamhâditthimânapapañka; in our verse by tamhâdisu papañkesu: cf. Lalita-vistara, p. 564, anâlayam nishprapañkam anutpâdam asambhavam (dharmakakram). As to Tathâgata, a name of Buddha, cf. Burnouf, Introd. p. 75.

255. Sankhâra for samskâra; cf. note to verse 203. Creature does not, as Mr. D'Alwis (p. 69) supposes, involve the Christian conception of creation.

CHAPTER XIX.

THE JUST.

256, 257. A man is not just if he carries a matter by violence ; no, he who distinguishes both right and wrong, who is learned and leads others, not by violence, but by law and equity, and who is guarded by the law and intelligent, he is called just.

258. A man is not learned because he talks much ; he who is patient, free from hatred and fear, he is called learned.

. 259. A man is not a supporter of the law because he talks much; even if a man has learnt little, but sees the law bodily, he is a supporter of the law, a man who never neglects the law.

260. A man is not an elder because his head is grey ; his age may be ripe, but he is called 'Old-in-vain.'

261. He in whom there is truth, virtue, love, restraint, moderation, he who is free from impurity and is wise, he is called an elder.   -

262. An envious, greedy, dishonest man does not become respectable by means of much talking only, or by the beauty of his complexion.

263. He in whom all this is destroyed, and taken out with the very root, he, when freed from hatred and wise, is called respectable.

---

259. Buddhaghosa here takes law (dhamma) in the sense of the four great truths, see note to verse 190. Could dhamma*m* káyena passati mean, 'he observes the law in his acts?' Hardly, if we compare expressions like dhamma*m* vipassato, v. 373.

264. Not by tonsure does an undisciplined man who speaks falsehood become a Samaṇa; can a man be a Samaṇa who is still held captive by desire and greediness?

265. He who always quiets the evil, whether small or large, he is called a Samaṇa (a quiet man), because he has quieted all evil.

266. A man is not a mendicant (Bhikshu) simply because he asks others for alms; he who adopts the whole law is a Bhikshu, not he who only begs.

267. He who is above good and evil, who is chaste, who with knowledge passes through the world, he indeed is called a Bhikshu.

268, 269. A man is not a Muni because he observes silence (mona, i. e. mauna), if he is foolish

---

265. This is a curious etymology, because it shows that at the time when this verse was written, the original meaning of *sramaṇa* had been forgotten. Sramaṇa meant originally, in the language of the Brahmans, a man who performed hard penances, from *sram*, 'to work hard,' &c. When it became the name of the Buddhist ascetics, the language had changed, and *sramaṇa* was pronounced samaṇa. Now there is another Sanskrit root, *sam*, 'to quiet,' which in Pâli becomes likewise sam, and from this root sam, 'to quiet,' and not from *sram*, 'to tire,' did the popular etymology of the day and the writer of our verse derive the title of the Buddhist priests. The original form *sramaṇa* became known to the Greeks as Σαρμάναι, that of samaṇa as Σαμαναῖοι; the former through Megasthenes, the latter through Bardesanes, 80–60 B.C. (See Lassen, Indische Alterthumskunde, II, 700.) The Chinese Shamen and the Tungusian Shamen come from the same source, though the latter has sometimes been doubted. See Schott, Über die doppelte Bedeutung des Wortes Schamane, in the Philosophical Transactions of the Berlin Academy, 1842, p. 463 seq.

266–270. The etymologies here given of the ordinary titles of the followers of Buddha are entirely fanciful, and are curious only as showing how the people who spoke Pâli had lost the etymological consciousness of their language. A Bhikshu is a beggar, and ignorant; but the wise who, taking the balance, chooses the good and avoids evil, he is a Muni, and is a Muni thereby; he who in this world weighs both sides is called a Muni.

270. A man is not an elect (Ariya) because he injures living creatures; because he has pity on all living creatures, therefore is a man called Ariya.

271, 272. Not only by discipline and vows, not only by much learning, not by entering into a trance, not by sleeping alone, do I earn the happiness of release which no worldling can know. Bhikshu, be not confident as long as thou hast not attained the extinction of desires.

---

i. e. a Buddhist friar who has left his family and lives entirely on alms.   Muni is a sage, hence Sâkya-muni, a name of Gautama. Muni comes from man, 'to think,' and from muni comes mauna, 'silence.'   Ariya, again, is the general name of those who embrace a religious life.   It meant originally 'respectable, noble.'   In verse 270 it seems as if the writer wished to guard against deriving ariya from ari, 'enemy.'   See note to verse 22.

272. See Childers, Notes, p. 7.

CHAPTER XX.

THE WAY.

273. The best of ways is the eightfold; the best of truths the four words; the best of virtues passionlessness; the best of men he who has eyes to see.

274. This is the way, there is no other that leads to the purifying of intelligence. Go on this way! Everything else is the deceit of Mâra (the tempter).

275. If you go on this way, you will make an end of pain! The way was preached by me, when I had understood the removal of the thorns (in the flesh).

276. You yourself must make an effort. The Tathâgatas (Buddhas) are only preachers. The thoughtful who enter the way are freed from the bondage of Mâra.

277. 'All created things perish,' he who knows and sees this becomes passive in pain; this is the way to purity.

---

273. The eightfold or eight-membered way is the technical term for the way by which Nirvâ*n*a is attained. (See Burnouf, Lotus, p. 519.) This very way constitutes the fourth of the Four Truths, or the four words of truth, viz. Du*h*kha, 'pain;' Samudaya, 'origin;' Nirodha, 'destruction;' Mârga, 'road.' (Lotus, p. 517.) See note to verse 178. For another explanation of the Mârga, or 'way,' see Hardy, Eastern Monachism, p. 280.

274. The last line may mean, 'this way is the confusion of Mâra,' i.e. the discomfiture of Mâra.

275. The *s*alyas, 'arrows or thorns,' are the *s*oka*s*alya, 'the arrows of grief.' Buddha himself is called mahâ*s*alya-hartâ, 'the great remover of thorns.' (Lalita-vistara, p. 550; Mahâbh. XII, 5616.)

277. See v. 255.

278. 'All created things are grief and pain,' he who knows and sees this becomes passive in pain ; this is the way that leads to purity.

279. 'All forms are unreal,' he who knows and sees this becomes passive in pain ; this is the way that leads to purity.

280. He who does not rouse himself when it is time to rise, who, though young and strong, is full of sloth, whose will and thought are weak, that lazy and idle man will never find the way to knowledge.

281. Watching his speech, well restrained in mind, let a man never commit any wrong with his body! Let a man but keep these three roads of action clear, and he will achieve the way which is taught by the wise.

282. Through zeal knowledge is gotten, through lack of zeal knowledge is lost ; let a man who knows this double path of gain and loss thus place himself that knowledge may grow.

283. Cut down the whole forest (of lust), not a tree only! Danger comes out of the forest (of lust). When you have cut down both the forest (of lust) and its undergrowth, then, Bhikshus, you will be rid of the forest and free!

---

278. See v. 203.

279. Dhamma is here explained, like saṅkhâra, as the five khandha, i. e. as what constitutes a living body.

281. Cf. Beal, Catena, p. 159.

282. Bhûri was rightly translated 'intelligentia' by Dr. Fausböll. Dr. Weber renders it by 'Gedeihen,' but the commentator distinctly explains it as 'vast knowledge,' and in the technical sense the word occurs after vidyâ and before medhâ, in the Lalita-vistara, p. 541.

283. A pun, vana meaning both 'lust' and 'forest.' See some mistaken remarks on this verse in D'Alwis, Nirvâna, p. 86, and some good remarks in Childers, Notes, p. 7.

284. So long as the love of man towards women, even the smallest, is not destroyed, so long is his mind in bondage, as the calf that drinks milk is to its mother.

285. Cut out the love of self, like an autumn lotus, with thy hand! Cherish the road of peace. Nirvâna has been shown by Sugata (Buddha).

286. ' Here I shall dwell in the rain, here in winter and summer,' thus the fool meditates, and does not think of his death.

287. Death comes and carries off that man, praised for his children and flocks, his mind distracted, as a flood carries off a sleeping village.

288. Sons are no help, nor a father, nor relations ; there is no help from kinsfolk for one whom death has seized.

289. A wise and good man who knows the meaning of this, should quickly clear the way that leads to Nirvâna.

---

285. Cf. Gâtaka, vol. i. p. 183.

286. Antarâya, according to the commentator, gîvitântarâya, i. e. interitus, death. In Sanskrit, antarita is used in the sense of ' vanished' or ' perished.'

287. See notes to verse 47, Thiessen, Kisâgotamî, p. 11, and Mahâbh. XII, 9944, 6540.

CHAPTER XXI.

MISCELLANEOUS.

290. If by leaving a small pleasure one sees a great pleasure, let a wise man leave the small pleasure, and look to the great.

291. He who, by causing pain to others, wishes to obtain pleasure for himself, he, entangled in the bonds of hatred, will never be free from hatred.

292. What ought to be done is neglected, what ought not to be done is done; the desires of unruly, thoughtless people are always increasing.

293. But they whose whole watchfulness is always directed to their body, who do not follow what ought not to be done, and who steadfastly do what ought to be done, the desires of such watchful and wise people will come to an end.

294. A true Brâhmaṇa goes scatheless, though he have killed father and mother, and two valiant kings, though he has destroyed a kingdom with all its subjects.

295. A true Brâhmaṇa goes scatheless, though he have killed father and mother, and two holy kings, and an eminent man besides.

---

292. Cf. Beal, Catena, p. 264.

294, 295. These two verses are either meant to show that a truly holy man who, by accident, commits all these crimes is guiltless, or they refer to some particular event in Buddha's history. The commentator is so startled that he explains them allegorically. Mr. D'Alwis is very indignant that I should have supposed Buddha capable of pardoning patricide. 'Can it be believed,' he writes, 'that a Teacher, who held life, even the life of the minutest insect,

296. The disciples of Gotama (Buddha) are always well awake, and their thoughts day and night are always set on Buddha.

297. The disciples of Gotama are always well awake, and their thoughts day and night are always set on the law.

298. The disciples of Gotama are always well awake, and their thoughts day and night are always set on the church.

299. The disciples of Gotama are always well awake, and their thoughts day and night are always set on their body.

---

nay, even a living tree, in such high estimation as to prevent its wanton destruction, has declared that the murder of a Brâhma*n*a, to whom he accorded reverence, along with his own Sangha, was blameless?' D'Alwis, Nirvâ*n*a, p. 88. Though something might be said in reply, considering the antecedents of king Agâta*s*atru, the patron of Buddha, and stories such as that quoted by the commentator on the Dhammapada (Beal, l.c. p. 150), or in Der Weise und der Thor, p. 306, still these two verses are startling, and I am not aware that Buddha has himself drawn the conclusion, which has been drawn by others, viz. that those who have reached the highest Sambodhi, and are in fact no longer themselves, are outside the domain of good and bad, and beyond the reach of guilt. Verses like 39 and 412 admit of a different explanation. Still our verses being miscellaneous extracts, might possibly have been taken from a work in which such an opinion was advanced, and I find that Mr. Childers, no mean admirer of Buddha, was not shocked by my explanation. 'In my judgment,' he says, 'this verse is intended to express in a forcible manner the Buddhist doctrine that the Arhat cannot commit a serious sin.' However, we have met before with far-fetched puns in these verses, and it is not impossible that the native commentators were right after all in seeing some puns or riddles in this verse. D'Alwis, following the commentary, explains mother as lust, father as pride, the two valiant kings as heretical systems, and the realm as sensual pleasure, while veyyaggha is taken by him for a place infested with the tigers of obstruction against final beatitude. Some confirmation of this interpretation is sup-

300. The disciples of Gotama are always well awake, and their mind day and night always delights in compassion.

301. The disciples of Gotama are always well awake, and their mind day and night always delights in meditation.

302. It is hard to leave the world (to become a friar), it is hard to enjoy the world; hard is the monastery, painful are the houses; painful it is to dwell with equals (to share everything in common), and the itinerant mendicant is beset with pain. Therefore let no man be an itinerant mendicant, and he will not be beset with pain.

303. Whatever place a faithful, virtuous, celebrated, and wealthy man chooses, there he is respected.

304. Good people shine from afar, like the snowy

plied by a passage in the third book of the Laṅkâvatâra-sûtra, as quoted by Mr. Beal in his translation of the Dhammapada, Introduction, p. 5. Here a stanza is quoted as having been recited by Buddha, in explanation of a similar startling utterance which he had made to Mahâmati:

'Lust, or carnal desire, this is the Mother,
Ignorance, this is the Father,
The highest point of knowledge, this is Buddha,
All the klesas, these are the Rahats,
The five skandhas, these are the Priests;
To commit the five unpardonable sins
Is to destroy these five
And yet not suffer the pains of hell.'

The Laṅkâvatâra-sûtra was translated into Chinese by Bodhiruki (508–511); when it was written is doubtful. See also Gâtaka, vol. ii. p. 263.

302. This verse is difficult, and I give my translation as tentative only. Childers (Notes, p. 11) does not remove the difficulties, and I have been chiefly guided by the interpretation put on the verse by the Chinese translator; Beal, Dhammapada, p. 137.

mountains; bad people are not seen, like arrows shot by night.

305. He alone who, without ceasing, practises the duty of sitting alone and sleeping alone, he, subduing himself, will rejoice in the destruction of all desires alone, as if living in a forest.

---

305. I have translated this verse so as to bring it into something like harmony with the preceding verses. Vanânte, according to a pun pointed out before (v. 283), means both 'in the end of a forest,' and 'in the end of desires.'

CHAPTER XXII.

THE DOWNWARD COURSE.

306. He who says what is not, goes to hell; he also who, having done a thing, says I have not done it. After death both are equal, they are men with evil deeds in the next world.

307. Many men whose shoulders are covered with the yellow gown are ill-conditioned and unrestrained; such evil-doers by their evil deeds go to hell.

308. Better it would be to swallow a heated iron ball, like flaring fire, than that a bad unrestrained fellow should live on the charity of the land.

309. Four things does a wreckless man gain who covets his neighbour's wife,—a bad reputation, an uncomfortable bed, thirdly, punishment, and lastly, hell.

---

306. I translate niraya, 'the exit, the downward course, the evil path,' by 'hell,' because the meaning assigned to that ancient mythological name by Christian writers comes so near to the Buddhist idea of niraya, that it is difficult not to believe in some actual contact between these two streams of thought.   See also Mahâbh. XII, 7176.   Cf. *G*âtaka, vol. ii. p. 416; Suttanipâta, v. 660.

307, 308. These two verses are said to be taken from the Vinaya-pi*t*aka I, 4, 1; D'Alwis, Nirvâ*n*a, p. 29.

308. The charity of the land, i. e. the alms given, from a sense of religious duty, to every mendicant that asks for it.

309, 310. The four things mentioned in verse 309 seem to be repeated in verse 310.   Therefore, apu*ññ*alâbha, 'bad fame,' is the same in both: gatî pâpikâ must be niraya; da*nd*a must be nindâ, and ratî thokikâ explains the anikâmaseyya*m*.   Buddhaghosa

310. There is bad reputation, and the evil way (to hell), there is the short pleasure of the frightened in the arms of the frightened, and the king imposes heavy punishment; therefore let no man think of his neighbour's wife.

311. As a grass-blade, if badly grasped, cuts the arm, badly-practised asceticism leads to hell.

312. An act carelessly performed, a broken vow, and hesitating obedience to discipline, all this brings no great reward.

313. If anything is to be done, let a man do it, let him attack it vigorously! A careless pilgrim only scatters the dust of his passions more widely.

314. An evil deed is better left undone, for a man repents of it afterwards; a good deed is better done, for having done it, one does not repent.

315. Like a well-guarded frontier fort, with defences within and without, so let a man guard himself. Not a moment should escape, for they who allow the right moment to pass, suffer pain when they are in hell.

316. They who are ashamed of what they ought not to be ashamed of, and are not ashamed of what they ought to be ashamed of, such men, embracing false doctrines, enter the evil path.

317. They who fear when they ought not to fear, and fear not when they ought to fear, such men, embracing false doctrines, enter the evil path.

---

takes the same view of the meaning of anikâmaseyya, i. e. yathâ ikkhati evam seyyam alabhitvâ, anikkhitam parittakam eva kâlam seyyam labhati, 'not obtaining the rest as he wishes it, he obtains it, as he does not wish it, for a short time only.'

313. As to raga meaning 'dust' and 'passion,' see Buddhaghosha's Parables, pp. 65, 66.

318. They who forbid when there is nothing to be forbidden, and forbid not when there is something to be forbidden, such men, embracing false doctrines, enter the evil path.

319. They who know what is forbidden as forbidden, and what is not forbidden as not forbidden, such men, embracing the true doctrine, enter the good path.

CHAPTER XXIII.

THE ELEPHANT.

320. Silently shall I endure abuse as the elephant in battle endures the arrow sent from the bow : for the world is ill-natured.

321. They lead a tamed elephant to battle, the king mounts a tamed elephant; the tamed is the best among men, he who silently endures abuse.

322. Mules are good, if tamed, and noble Sindhu horses, and elephants with large tusks ; but he who tames himself is better still.

323. For with these animals does no man reach the untrodden country (Nirvâ*n*a), where a tamed man goes on a tamed animal, viz. on his own well-tamed self.

324. The elephant called Dhanapâlaka, his temples running with sap, and difficult to hold, does not eat a morsel when bound; the elephant longs for the elephant grove.

320. The elephant is with the Buddhists the emblem of endurance and self-restraint. Thus Buddha himself is called Nâga, 'the Elephant' (Lal. Vist. p. 553), or Mahânâga, 'the great Elephant' (Lal. Vist. p. 553), and in one passage (Lal. Vist. p. 554) the reason of this name is given, by stating that Buddha was sudânta, 'well-tamed,' like an elephant. He descended from heaven in the form of an elephant to be born on earth.

Cf. Manu VI, 47, ativâdâ*m*s titiksheta.

323. I read, as suggested by Dr. Fausböll, yath' attanâ sudantena danto dantena ga*kkh*ati' (cf. verse 160). The India Office MS. reads na hi etehi *th*ânehi ga*kkh*eya agata*m* disam, yath' attâna*m* sudantena danto dantena ga*kkh*ati. As to *th*ânehi instead of yânehi, see verse 224.

325. If a man becomes fat and a great eater, if he is sleepy and rolls himself about, that fool, like a hog fed on wash, is born again and again.

326. This mind of mine went formerly wandering about as it liked, as it listed, as it pleased; but I shall now hold it in thoroughly, as the rider who holds the hook holds in the furious elephant.

327. Be not thoughtless, watch your thoughts! Draw yourself out of the evil way, like an elephant sunk in mud.

328. If a man find a prudent companion who walks with him, is wise, and lives soberly, he may walk with him, overcoming all dangers, happy, but considerate.

329. If a man find no prudent companion who walks with him, is wise, and lives soberly, let him walk alone, like a king who has left his conquered country behind,—like an elephant in the forest.

330. It is better to live alone, there is no companionship with a fool; let a man walk alone, let him commit no sin, with few wishes, like an elephant in the forest.

---

326. Yoniso, i.e. yoniśaḥ, is rendered by Dr. Fausböll ' sapientiâ,' and this is the meaning ascribed to yoni by many Buddhist authorities. But the reference to Hemaḱandra (ed. Boehtlingk and Rieu, p. 281) shows clearly that it meant 'origin,' or 'cause.' Yoniso occurs frequently as a mere adverb, meaning ' thoroughly, radically' (Dhammapada, p. 359), and yoniso manasikâra (Dhammapada, p. 110) means ' taking to heart' or ' minding thoroughly,' or, what is nearly the same, 'wisely.' In the Lalita-vistara, p. 41, the commentator has clearly mistaken yoniśaḥ, changing it to ye 'niśo, and explaining it by yamaniśam, whereas M. Foucaux has rightly translated it by ' depuis l'origine.' Professor Weber suspected in yoniśaḥ a double entendre, but even grammar would show that our author is innocent of it. In Lalita-vistara, p. 544, l. 4, ayoniśa occurs in the sense of error.

328, 329. Cf. Suttanipâta, vv. 44, 45.

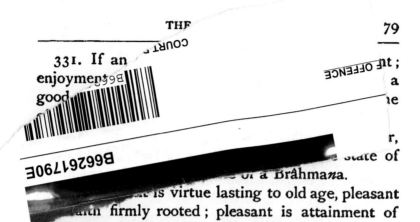

331. If an
enjoyment
good

THE OFFENCE ... nt ;
a
ie

r,
... state of
... of a Brâhma*n*a.

... is virtue lasting to old age, pleasant
... firmly rooted ; pleasant is attainment of
intelligence, pleasant is avoiding of sins.

33ᵃ. The commentator throughout takes these words, like mat-
teyyatâ, &c., to signify, not the status of a mother, or maternity,
but reverence shown to a mother.

CHAPTER XXIV.

THIRST.

334. The thirst of a thoughtless man grows like a creeper ; he runs from life to life, like a monkey seeking fruit in the forest.

335. Whomsoever this fierce thirst overcomes, full of poison, in this world, his sufferings increase like the abounding Bîrana grass.

336. He who overcomes this fierce thirst, difficult to be conquered in this world, sufferings fall off from him, like water-drops from a lotus leaf.

337. This salutary word I tell you, 'Do ye, as many as are here assembled, dig up the root of thirst, as he who wants the sweet-scented Usîra root must dig up the Bîrana grass, that Mâra (the tempter) may not crush you again and again, as the stream crushes the reeds.'

338. As a tree, even though it has been cut down, is firm so long as its root is safe, and grows again, thus, unless the feeders of thirst are destroyed, this pain (of life) will return again and again.

339. He whose thirst running towards pleasure is exceeding strong in the thirty-six channels, the

---

334. This is explained by a story in the Chinese translation. Beal, Dhammapada, p. 148.

335. Bîrana grass is the Andropogon muricatum, and the scented root of it is called Usîra (cf. verse 337).

338. On Anusaya, i. e. Anusaya (Anlage), see Wassiljew, Der Buddhismus, p. 240 seq.

339. The thirty-six channels, or passions, which are divided by the commentator into eighteen external and eighteen internal, are

waves will carry away that misguided man, viz. his desires which are set on passion.

340. The channels run everywhere, the creeper (of passion) stands sprouting ; if you see the creeper springing up, cut its root by means of knowledge.

341. A creature's pleasures are extravagant and luxurious; sunk in lust and looking for pleasure, men undergo (again and again) birth and decay.

342. Men, driven on by thirst, run about like a snared hare; held in fetters and bonds, they undergo pain for a long time, again and again.

343. Men, driven on by thirst, run about like a snared hare; let therefore the mendicant drive out thirst, by striving after passionlessness for himself.

344. He who having got rid of the forest (of lust) (i.e. after having reached Nirvâna) gives himself over to forest-life (i.e. to lust), and who, when removed from the forest (i.e. from lust), runs to the forest (i.e. to lust), look at that man! though free, he runs into bondage.

---

explained by Burnouf (Lotus, p. 649), from a gloss of the Ginaalankâra : 'L'indication précise des affections dont un Buddha acte indépendant, affections qui sont au nombre de dix-huit, nous est fourni par la glose d'un livre appartenant aux Buddhistes de Ceylan,' &c. Subhûti gives the right reading as manâpassavanâ ; cf. Childers, Notes, p. 12.

Vâhâ, which Dr. Fausböll translates by 'equi,' may be vahâ, 'undae.' Cf. Suttanipâta, v. 1034.

344. This verse seems again full of puns, all connected with the twofold meaning of vana, 'forest and lust.' By replacing 'forest' by 'lust,' we may translate : 'He who, when free from lust, gives himself up to lust, who, when removed from lust runs into lust, look at that man,' &c. Nibbana, though with a short a, may be intended to remind the hearer of Nibbâna. The right reading is nibbanatho; see Childers, Notes, p. 8.

345. Wise people do not call that a strong fetter which is made of iron, wood, or hemp; far stronger is the care for precious stones and rings, for sons and a wife.

346. That fetter wise people call strong which drags down, yields, but is difficult to undo; after having cut this at last, people leave the world, free from cares, and leaving desires and pleasures behind.

347. Those who are slaves to passions, run down with the stream (of desires), as a spider runs down the web which he has made himself; when they have cut this, at last, wise people leave the world, free from cares, leaving all affection behind.

348. Give up what is before, give up what is behind, give up what is in the middle, when thou goest to the other shore of existence; if thy mind is altogether free, thou wilt not again enter into birth and decay.

349. If a man is tossed about by doubts, full of strong passions, and yearning only for what is delightful, his thirst will grow more and more, and he will indeed make his fetters strong.

350. If a man delights in quieting doubts, and, always reflecting, dwells on what is not delightful

---

345. Apekhâ, apekshâ, 'care;' see Manu VI, 41, 49; Suttani-pâta, v. 37; and Gâtaka, vol. ii. p. 140.

346. Paribbag, i. e. parivrag; see Manu VI, 41.

347. The commentator explains the simile of the spider as follows: 'As a spider, after having made its thread-web, sits in the middle, and after killing with a violent rush a butterfly or a fly which has fallen in its circle, drinks its juice, returns, and sits again in the same place, in the same manner creatures who are given to passions, depraved by hatred, and maddened by wrath, run along the stream of thirst which they have made themselves, and cannot cross it,' &c.

(the impurity of the body, &c.), he certainly will remove, nay, he will cut the fetter of Mâra.

351. He who has reached the consummation, who does not tremble, who is without thirst and without sin, he has broken all the thorns of life : this will be his last body.

352. He who is without thirst and without affection, who understands the words and their interpretation, who knows the order of letters (those which are before and which are after), he has received his last body, he is called the great sage, the great man.

353. 'I have conquered all, I know all, in all conditions of life I am free from taint ; I have left all, and through the destruction of thirst I am free ;. having learnt myself, whom shall I teach ?'

354. The gift of the law exceeds all gifts ; the sweetness of the law exceeds all sweetness ; the delight in the law exceeds all delights ; the extinction of thirst overcomes all pain.

355. Pleasures destroy the foolish, if they look not for the other shore ; the foolish by his thirst for pleasures destroys himself, as if he were his own enemy.

---

352. As to nirutti, and its technical meaning among the Buddhists, see Burnouf, Lotus, p. 841. Fausböll translates 'niruttis vocabulorum peritus,' which may be right, if we take nirutti in the sense of the language of the Scriptures. See note to verse 363. Could not sannipâta mean samhitâ or sannikarsha ? Sannipâta occurs in the Sâkala-prâtisâkhya, but with a different meaning.

353. Cf. Suttanipâta, v. 210.

354. The dhammadâna, or 'gift of the law,' is the technical term for instruction in the Buddhist religion. See Buddhaghosha's Parables, p. 160, where the story of the Sakkadevarâga is told, and where a free rendering of our verse is given.

356. The fields are damaged by weeds, mankind is damaged by passion : therefore a gift bestowed on the passionless brings great reward.

357. The fields are damaged by weeds, mankind is damaged by hatred : therefore a gift bestowed on those who do not hate brings great reward.

358. The fields are damaged by weeds, mankind is damaged by vanity : therefore a gift bestowed on those who are free from vanity brings great reward.

359. The fields are damaged by weeds, mankind is damaged by lust : therefore a gift bestowed on those who are free from lust brings great reward.

CHAPTER XXV.

THE BHIKSHU (MENDICANT).

360. Restraint in the eye is good, good is restraint in the ear, in the nose restraint is good, good is restraint in the tongue.

361. In the body restraint is good, good is restraint in speech, in thought restraint is good, good is restraint in all things. A Bhikshu, restrained in all things, is freed from all pain.

362. He who controls his hand, he who controls his feet, he who controls his speech, he who is well controlled, he who delights inwardly, who is collected, who is solitary and content, him they call Bhikshu.

363. The Bhikshu who controls his mouth, who speaks wisely and calmly, who teaches the meaning and the law, his word is sweet.

364. He who dwells in the law, delights in the law, meditates on the law, follows the law, that Bhikshu will never fall away from the true law.

365. Let him not despise what he has received,

---

363. On artha and dharma, see Stanislas Julien, Les Avadânas, I, 217, note; 'Les quatre connaissances sont; 1º la connaissance du sens (artha); 2º la connaissance de la Loi (dharma); 3º la connaissance des explications (niroukti); 4º la connaissance de l'intelligence (prâtibhâna).'

364. The expression dhammârâmo, 'having his garden or delight (Lustgarten) in the law,' is well matched by the Brahmanic expression ekârâma, i. e. nirdvandva (Mahâbh. XIII, 1930). Cf. Suttanipâta, v. 326; Dhammapada, v. 32.

nor ever envy others: a mendicant who envies
others does not obtain peace of mind.

366. A Bhikshu who, though he receives little,
does not despise what he has received, even the
gods will praise him, if his life is pure, and if he is
not slothful.

367. He who never identifies himself with name
and form, and does not grieve over what is no more,
he indeed is called a Bhikshu.

368. The Bhikshu who acts with kindness, who is
calm in the doctrine of Buddha, will reach the quiet
place (Nirvâna), cessation of natural desires, and
happiness.

369. O Bhikshu, empty this boat! if emptied, it
will go quickly; having cut off passion and hatred,
thou wilt go to Nirvâna.

370. Cut off the five (senses), leave the five, rise
above the five. A Bhikshu, who has escaped from
the five fetters, he is called Oghatinna, 'saved from
the flood.'

371. Meditate, O Bhikshu, and be not heedless!
Do not direct thy thought to what gives pleasure,
that thou mayest not for thy heedlessness have to
swallow the iron ball (in hell), and that thou mayest
not cry out when burning, ' This is pain.'

---

367. Nâmarûpa is here used again in its technical sense of
mind and body, neither of which, however, is with the Buddhists
âtman, or 'self.' Asat, 'what is not,' may therefore mean the same
as nâmarûpa, or we may take it in the sense of what is no more,
as, for instance, the beauty or youth of the body, the vigour of the
mind, &c.

368. See Childers, Notes, p. 11.

371. The swallowing of hot iron balls is considered as a punishment in hell; see verse 308. Professor Weber has perceived the

372. Without knowledge there is no meditation, without meditation there is no knowledge: he who has knowledge and meditation is near unto Nirvâna.

373. A Bhikshu who has entered his empty house, and whose mind is tranquil, feels a more than human delight when he sees the law clearly.

374. As soon as he has considered the origin and destruction of the elements (khandha) of the body, he finds happiness and joy which belong to those who know the immortal (Nirvâna).

375. And this is the beginning here for a wise Bhikshu: watchfulness over the senses, contentedness, restraint under the law; keep noble friends whose life is pure, and who are not slothful.

376. Let him live in charity, let him be perfect in his duties; then in the fulness of delight he will make an end of suffering.

377. As the Vassikâ plant sheds its withered flowers, men should shed passion and hatred, O ye Bhikshus!

378. The Bhikshu whose body and tongue and mind are quieted, who is collected, and has rejected the baits of the world, he is called quiet.

379. Rouse thyself by thyself, examine thyself by thyself, thus self-protected and attentive wilt thou live happily, O Bhikshu!

380. For self is the lord of self, self is the refuge of self; therefore curb thyself as the merchant curbs a good horse.

---

right meaning of bhavassu, which can only be bhâvayasva, but I doubt whether the rest of his rendering is right, for who would swallow an iron ball by accident?

372. Cf. Beal, Catena, p. 247.
375. Cf. Suttanipâta, v. 337.

381. The Bhikshu, full of delight, who is calm in the doctrine of Buddha will reach the quiet place (Nirvâna), cessation of natural desires, and happiness.

382. He who, even as a young Bhikshu, applies himself to the doctrine of Buddha, brightens up this world, like the moon when free from clouds.

---

381. See verse 368.   D'Alwis translates, ' dissolution of the sankhâras (elements of existence).'

CHAPTER XXVI.

THE BRÂHMANA (ARHAT).

383. Stop the stream valiantly, drive away the desires, O Brâhmana! When you have understood the destruction of all that was made, you will understand that which was not made.

384. If the Brâhmana has reached the other shore in both laws (in restraint and contemplation), all bonds vanish from him who has obtained knowledge.

385. He for whom there is neither this nor that shore, nor both, him, the fearless and unshackled, I call indeed a Brâhmana.

386. He who is thoughtful, blameless, settled, dutiful, without passions, and who has attained the highest end, him I call indeed a Brâhmana.

387. The sun is bright by day, the moon shines by night, the warrior is bright in his armour, the Brâhmana is bright in his meditation; but Buddha, the Awakened, is bright with splendour day and night.

388. Because a man is rid of evil, therefore he is called Brâhmana; because he walks quietly, therefore he is called Samana; because he has sent away his own impurities, therefore he is called Pravragita (Pabbagita, a pilgrim).

---

385. The exact meaning of the two shores is not quite clear, and the commentator who takes them in the sense of internal and external organs of sense, can hardly be right. See verse 86.

388. These would-be etymologies are again interesting as showing the decline of the etymological life of the spoken language of

[10]　　　　k

389. No one should attack a Brâhmaṇa, but no Brâhmaṇa (if attacked) should let himself fly at his aggressor! Woe to him who strikes a Brâhmaṇa, more woe to him who flies at his aggressor!

390. It advantages a Brâhmaṇa not a little if he holds his mind back from the pleasures of life ; when all wish to injure has vanished, pain will cease.

391. Him I call indeed a Brâhmaṇa who does not offend by body, word, or thought, and is controlled on these three points.

392. After a man has once understood the law as taught by the Well-awakened (Buddha), let him worship it carefully, as the Brâhmaṇa worships the sacrificial fire.

393. A man does not become a Brâhmaṇa by his platted hair, by his family, or by birth ; in whom there is truth and righteousness, he is blessed, he is a Brâhmaṇa.

394. What is the use of platted hair, O fool! what of the raiment of goat-skins ? Within thee there is ravening, but the outside thou makest clean.

395. The man who wears dirty raiments, who is

India at the time when such etymologies became possible. In order to derive Brâhmaṇa from vâh, it must have been pronounced bâhmaṇo ; vâh, 'to remove,' occurs frequently in the Buddhistical Sanskrit. Cf. Lal.Vist. p. 551, l. 1 ; 553, l. 7. See note to verse 265.

390. I am afraid I have taken too much liberty with this verse. Dr. Fausböll translates, ' Non Brâhmaṇae hoc paulo melius, quando retentio fit mentis a jucundis.'

393. Fausböll proposes to read gakkâ (gâtyâ). 'Both' in the first edition of my translation was a misprint for 'birth.'

394. I have not copied the language of the Bible more than I was justified in. The words are abbhantaran te gahanaṃ, bâhiraṃ parimaggasi, 'interna est abyssus, externum mundas.' Cf. Gâtaka, vol. i. p. 481.

395. The expression Kisaṃ dhamanisanthataṃ is the Sanskrit

emaciated and covered with veins, who lives alone in the forest, and meditates, him I call indeed a Brâhmana.

396. I do not call a man a Brâhmana because of his origin or of his mother. He is indeed arrogant, and he is wealthy: but the poor, who is free from all attachments, him I call indeed a Brâhmana.

397. Him I call indeed a Brâhmana who has cut all fetters, who never trembles, is independent and unshackled.

398. Him I call indeed a Brâhmana who has cut the strap and the thong, the chain with all that pertains to it, who has burst the bar, and is awakened.

399. Him I call indeed a Brâhmana who, though he has committed no offence, endures reproach, bonds, and stripes, who has endurance for his force, and strength for his army.

400. Him I call indeed a Brâhmana who is free from anger, dutiful, virtuous, without appetite, who is subdued, and has received his last body.

krisam dhamanîsantatam, the frequent occurrence of which in the Mahâbhârata has been pointed out by Boehtlingk, s. v. dhamani. It looks more like a Brâhmanic than like a Buddhist phrase.

396. From verse 396 to the first half of verse 423, the text of the Dhammapada agrees with the text of the Vasishtha-Bharadvâgasûtra. These verses are translated by D'Alwis in his Nirvâna, pp. 113-118, and again by Fausböll, Suttanipâta, v. 620 seq. The text contains puns on kiñkana, which means 'wealth,' but also 'attachment;' cf. Childers, s. v.

398. D'Alwis points out a double entendre in these words. Nandhi may be either the strap that goes round a drum, or enmity; varatta may be either a thong or attachment; sandâna either chain or scepticism; sahanakkamam either due order or all its concomitants; paligha either bar or ignorance.

399. The exact meaning of balânîka is difficult to find. Does it mean, possessed of a strong army, or facing a force, or leading a force?

k 2

401. Him I call indeed a Brâhmaṇa who does not cling to pleasures, like water on a lotus leaf, like a mustard seed on the point of a needle.

402. Him I call indeed a Brâhmaṇa who, even here, knows the end of his suffering, has put down his burden, and is unshackled.

403. Him I call indeed a Brâhmaṇa whose knowledge is deep, who possesses wisdom, who knows the right way and the wrong, and has attained the highest end.

404. Him I call indeed a Brâhmaṇa who keeps aloof both from laymen and from mendicants, who frequents no houses, and has but few desires.

405. Him I call indeed a Brâhmaṇa who finds no fault with other beings, whether feeble or strong, and does not kill nor cause slaughter.

406. Him I call indeed a Brâhmaṇa who is tolerant with the intolerant, mild with fault-finders, and free from passion among the passionate.

407. Him I call indeed a Brâhmaṇa from whom anger and hatred, pride and envy have dropt like a mustard seed from the point of a needle.

408. Him I call indeed a Brâhmaṇa who utters true speech, instructive and free from harshness, so that he offend no one.

409. Him I call indeed a Brâhmaṇa who takes nothing in the world that is not given him, be it long or short, small or large, good or bad.

410. Him I call indeed a Brâhmaṇa who fosters no desires for this world or for the next, has no inclinations, and is unshackled.

---

405. On tasa and thâvara, see Childers, s. v., and D'Alwis, Nirvâna, p. 115. On daṇḍa, 'the rod,' see Hibbert Lectures, p. 355, note.

411. Him I call indeed a Brâhmana who has no interests, and when he has understood (the truth), does not say How, how? and who has reached the depth of the Immortal.

412. Him I call indeed a Brâhmana who in this world is above good and evil, above the bondage of both, free from grief, from sin, and from impurity.

413. Him I call indeed a Brâhmana who is bright like the moon, pure, serene, undisturbed, and in whom all gaiety is extinct.

414. Him I call indeed a Brâhmana who has traversed this miry road, the impassable world and its vanity, who has gone through, and reached the other shore, is thoughtful, guileless, free from doubts, free from attachment, and content.

415. Him I call indeed a Brâhmana who in this world, leaving all desires, travels about without a home, and in whom all concupiscence is extinct.

416. Him I call indeed a Brâhmana who, leaving all longings, travels about without a home, and in whom all covetousness is extinct.

417. Him I call indeed a Brâhmana who, after leaving all bondage to men, has risen above all

---

411. Akathankathi is explained by Buddhaghosa as meaning, 'free from doubt or hesitation.' He also uses kathankathâ in the sense of 'doubt' (verse 414). In the Kâvyâdarsa, III, 17, the commentator explains akatham by kathârahitam, nirvivâdam, which would mean, 'without a kathâ, a speech, a story without contradiction, unconditionally.' From our passage, however, it seems as if kathankathâ was a noun derived from kathankathayati, 'to say How, how?' so that neither the first nor the second element had anything to do with kath, 'to relate;' and in that case akatham, too, ought to be taken in the sense of 'without a Why.'

412. See verse 39. The distinction between good and evil vanishes when a man has retired from the world, and has ceased to act, longing only for deliverance.

bondage to the gods, and is free from all and every bondage.

418. Him I call indeed a Brâhma*n*a who has left what gives pleasure and what gives pain, who is cold, and free from all germs (of renewed life), the hero who has conquered all the worlds.

419. Him I call indeed a Brâhma*n*a who knows the destruction and the return of beings everywhere, who is free from bondage, welfaring (Sugata), and awakened (Buddha).

418. Upadhi, if not used in a technical sense, is best translated by 'passions or affections.' Technically there are four upadhis or substrata, viz. the kandhas, kâma, 'desire,' kilesa, 'sin,' and kamma, 'work.' The Brâhma*n*a may be called nirupadhi, as being free from desire, misery, and work and its consequences, but not yet of the kandhas, which end through death only. The commentator explains nirupadhi by nirupakkilesa, 'free from sin.' See Childers, s. v. nibbâna, p. 268 a.

419. Sugata is one of those many words in Buddhist literature which it is almost impossible to translate, because they have been taken in so many acceptations by the Buddhists themselves. Sugata etymologically means 'one who has fared well,' sugati means 'happiness and blessedness.' It is wrong to translate it literally by 'welcome,' for that in Sanskrit is svâgata; and we cannot accept Dr. Eitel's statement (Handbook, p. 138) that sugata stands incorrectly for svâgata. Sugata is one of the not very numerous technical terms in Buddhism for which hitherto we know of no antecedents in earlier Brahmanism. It may have been used in the sense of 'happy and blessed,' but it never became a title, while in Buddhism it has become, not only a title, but almost a proper name of Buddha. The same applies to tathâgata, lit. 'thus come,' but used in Sanskrit very much like tathâvidha, in the sense of talis, while in Buddhism it means a Buddha. There are of course many interpretations of the word, and many reasons are given why Buddhas should be called Tathâgata (Burnouf, Introduction, p. 75, &c.) Boehtlingk s. v. supposed that, because Buddha had so many predicates, he was, for the sake of brevity, called 'such a one as he really is.' I think we may go a step further. Another word, tâd*r*isa, meaning

420. Him I call indeed a Brâhmaña whose path the gods do not know, nor spirits (Gandharvas), nor men, whose passions are extinct, and who is an Arhat (venerable).

421. Him I call indeed a Brâhmaña who calls nothing his own, whether it be before, behind, or between, who is poor, and free from the love of the world.

422. Him I call indeed a Brâhmaña, the manly, the noble, the hero, the great sage, the conqueror, the impassible, the accomplished, the awakened.

423. Him I call indeed a Brâhmaña who knows his former abodes, who sees heaven and hell, has reached the end of births, is perfect in knowledge, a sage, and whose perfections are all perfect.

Rules Biel 2992 = 10 $\frac{7}{17}$ 45%